Warrior

of

Peace

Warrior

of

Peace

KIM MICHAELS

Copyright © 2015 Kim Michaels. All rights reserved. No part of this book may be used, reproduced, translated, electronically stored or transmitted by any means except by written permission from the publisher. A reviewer may quote brief passages in a review.

MORE TO LIFE PUBLISHING

www.morepublish.com

For foreign and translation rights,
contact info@ morepublish.com

ISBN: 978-87-93297-08-1

The information and insights in this book should not be considered as a form of therapy, advice, direction, diagnosis, and/or treatment of any kind. This information is not a substitute for medical, psychological, or other professional advice, counseling and care. All matters pertaining to your individual health should be supervised by a physician or appropriate health-care practitioner. No guarantee is made by the author or the publisher that the practices described in this book will yield successful results for anyone at any time. They are presented for informational purposes only, as the practice and proof rests with the individual.

For the spiritual tools recommended by the Master, see:
www.transcendencetoolbox.com

CONTENTS

1 | The Reluctant Student 7
2 | The Central Human Dilemma 17
3 | The Warrior Discovers His Life Goal 35
4 | Seeing the "Enemy" Within 45
5 | The Subtle Workings of the Human Mind 57
6 | Freedom from Anger and Guilt 79
7 | Freedom from Value Judgments 87
8 | The Seven Beasts 103
9 | The Lion and the Snake 113
10 | The Wolf and the Caribou 119
11 | The Sea Monster and the Jelly Fish 123
12 | The Hawk and the Spider 127
13 | The Tiger and the Monkey 133
14 | The Cobra and the Rat 141
15 | Why Nations Go to War 147
16 | How the Machine Keeps People Trapped 171
17 | The Human Dilemma Revisited 177
18 | The Pieces and the Puzzle 193
19 | The Warrior Surrenders the Warrior 207
20 | The Warrior Leaves and Returns 219

1 | THE RELUCTANT STUDENT

The Warrior's first meeting with the Master

The Master is walking in the marketplace with his closest student. The Warrior is marching down the road, his mind set on battle. When he meets the Master and his student, the Master says: 'My Son, where are you going with such fierce determination?'

The Warrior answers: 'The enemy has attacked our nation. He has destroyed two of our tallest buildings and taken away our peace. I go to destroy the enemy and bring back peace!'

The Master asks: 'My Son, if the enemy took away peace through violence, how can more violence bring back peace?'

The Warrior declares: 'There is no other way. When the enemy is destroyed, peace will return!'

The Master replies: 'My Son, I perceive that your heart is troubled. It is filled with anger and hatred towards the enemy. Might it be the anger and hatred that has taken away peace?'

The Warrior says: 'The enemy created the anger. Once the enemy is destroyed, the hatred will be gone and peace will return!'

The Master tries again: 'My Son, if the enemy caused your anger, then the enemy must rule your inner world. Perhaps you could conquer the enemy within before you do battle with the enemy without? Perhaps you could find peace in your heart before you attempt to bring peace to the world?'

The Warrior declares: 'I cannot find peace until the enemy is destroyed!' Then he marches on without looking back.

The Master smiles gently and walks on. His student exclaims: 'Master, he did not understand your wisdom and is headed for his own destruction. How can you seem so unconcerned? Let us run after him and save him from himself!'

The Master replies: 'My dearest student, if I preach inner peace, how can I let my own peace be disturbed by someone rejecting my message?'

'Besides, while his body might be destroyed, his soul and spirit will live on. One day the soul will tire of trying to bring peace by fighting outer enemies. It will discover the enemy within, and eventually it will discover the inner source of peace.'

'While we can seek to help others learn their lessons, we must never seek to force them. After all, we cannot learn their lessons for them. They must learn them through their own, inner experiences.'

'Peace cannot be brought through force. Conflict is the absence of peace. Peace cannot be brought by removing conflict. *Outer* peace can be brought only through *inner* peace. The only way to bring peace is to *be* peace wherever there is non-peace. Let us begin with ourselves, my dear student!'

1 | The Reluctant Student

The Warrior's second meeting with the master

Seasons pass, clouds are flung across the skies, flowers bloom and wither, much water runs through the great rivers into the oceans.

The Master is walking through the marketplace with several students. They come upon a man with long hair and beard who is sitting on the sidewalk with a begging bowl. He is missing one leg from the knee down. His face is disfigured by an angry expression and he yells profanities at those who pass by without leaving anything in his bowl. He grunts angrily at those who do leave a coin. The students start turning away, but the Master walks up to the man: 'My Son, I see you have returned. Were you successful in your quest for destroying the enemy and bringing back peace?'

The Warrior looks up with an angry expression, then pauses and a light of recognition sparks in his eyes. He looks down, and after some time replies: 'I remember you, old man. You told me not to go. I should have listened, then neither my body nor my soul would have been shattered ...'

The Warrior starts weeping silently, and after some time he says: 'The enemy attacked us. Our leader called for those who would go destroy the enemy. I volunteered, thinking I could make a difference. I trained for many months, but when I was sent into battle, I was unprepared for the reality of what it is like to kill or be killed.'

'Still, I pressed on. I killed my own fear. I killed my own emotions. I killed my own humanity. I became the perfect killing machine, driven by hatred of the enemy to conquer all obstacles. I became so good at killing that I felt I was invincible and could never be hurt myself. Yet as the killing went on, I saw things that no human should have to see. I saw that the killing could not always be justified. I saw that in the fog of war, we killed those who had not attacked us, those who had no hatred towards us. We killed those who just wanted to live their lives on their own terms, which is exactly what our nation takes pride in allowing its citizens to do.'

'I began to feel that I had been fooled into going to war without understanding that I was just an insignificant cog in a huge machine. I started seeing the political machine aimed at controlling the world, with no concern whatsoever for the individuals being killed and maimed by the grinding wheels of the Machine.'

'One day, I was trying to help a wounded soldier when a cowardly bomb planted by the enemy blew off my leg. As I was lying there, thinking I would bleed to death, I felt I had been let down by life, by luck, by my country and by God. I cursed them all. I cursed life, I cursed Lady Luck, I cursed the Machine, I cursed my country and I even cursed God.'

'I then felt an inner peace, and I looked forward to dying. I felt the life force ebbing out of my body, and I looked forward to melting away into nothingness. After I lost consciousness, a medical unit picked me up and two days later I woke up in a field hospital with no leg and no future.'

'I was sent back to the country of my birth, but it was no longer home. I was offered assistance, but no one could understand what I had gone through. No one could help me deal with the anger of being alive when I wanted to be dead. I know that because I cursed God, he decided to punish me by keeping me alive so I would live many years in this miserable condition, neither fully man nor fully a crawling animal.'

'Yes, I was angry and I attempted to make everyone I met as miserable as myself. I rejected every hand extended to me, and now I sit here on the street, begging for money to buy food to sustain this miserable body that has become the most cruel of prisons. And it is all because nobody cares.'

1 | The Reluctant Student

'My country is run by the Machine and it does not care about the individual. My countrymen just want to live their comfortable lives and have us fight for their freedom to do so. Nobody cares about me, nobody cares ... *nobody freaking cares!!!*' The Warrior yells at a passing businessman in an impersonal suit.

The Master says: 'My Son, you said that you should have listened to me when we first met. Do you perhaps see why you did not listen to me?'

The Warrior answers: 'I have no idea, old man. Why don't you tell me, since you seem to have all the answers.'

'When we first met,' the Master replies, 'your mind was firmly set on your perception that you had to bring back peace by destroying the enemy. You were not open to anything I said. Now your mind is just as firmly set on your perception that nobody cares about you. My question is: Are you willing to put that perception to the test?'

'What perception,' the Warrior says angrily, 'this is not a freaking perception. *It's a fact!* Nobody cares about anybody. The world is run by this huge machine that makes everybody do something because they think they will get something for themselves. Nobody does something without a selfish motive, so what's yours, old man?'

'My Son, one thing I have learned over the years is that what seems like a fact from one perspective will seem like unreality from a higher perspective. I ask again: Are you willing to put your "fact" to the test?'

'And just how would I do that?'

'My students and I live in a modest ashram not far from here. I will offer you a roof over your head, a bed to sleep on and three meals a day for as long as you care to stay.'

'And what is the catch, what do you want in return, what do you get from me for doing that? I am not going to listen to any of your teachings. I have already had the psychologists give me all of their psycho-babble and none of it worked on me. I am way beyond help, they told me, so don't you think you can fix me, 'cause I don't wanna be fixed, old man. I just wanna live out my miserable existence until God decides I have suffered enough and calls it quits.'

'Perhaps,' the Master answers with a glint in his eye, 'the reward I seek is to hear your voice yelling at my students.'

'Fine then,' the Warrior answers, 'let's give it a go. I'll bet you throw me out after a week anyway.'

The Master and his students help the Warrior into his wheelchair and take him back to the Ashram where they install him in a small room.

The students complain to the Master

Several weeks pass. The Warrior refuses to leave his room. When the students bring him food, he yells at them and curses them. He goes to the bathroom by himself but refuses to take showers or clean his room. One day, the students gather around the Master, and the oldest student asks:

'Master, we want to ask why you keep the Warrior here. He does not seem to be changing. He is angry and abusive towards us no matter what we try to do for him. He has no interest in your teachings or our purpose for living in this ashram. Why is he here when he only disturbs the peace we knew before he came?'

The Master looks at the students with a loving expression, then says: 'My students, the Warrior is here partly for *his* testing and partly for *our* testing.'

'Master, what do you mean?,' asks one student.

1 | The Reluctant Student

The Master answers: 'The Warrior is here partly because while you had peace before he came, it was not ultimate peace. The Warrior is the ultimate teacher who is here to teach you something about peace that you cannot learn from me.'

'But Master,' says another student, 'you have attained inner peace so you would be the ultimate teacher of peace. The Warrior has no inner peace so how can he teach us to attain what he does not have himself? We are confused, Master.'

The Master asks: 'What is it I seek to teach you?'

'You seek to teach us how to attain inner peace so we can help bring peace to the world.'

'No,' replies the Master, 'inner peace is only an effect, as is world peace. What is the cause of inner peace?'

The students look confused and the Master continues: 'Individual peace is an effect of self-mastery. World peace is an effect of a critical mass of people attaining self-mastery.'

'I am not seeking to teach you inner peace. I am seeking to teach you how to master the inner world of your own minds so that nothing from within or without can take away your peace.'

'In order for you to attain this, you must master your own reactions to the world and to other people. The Warrior is here to help you master your reactions to him. When you master your reactions so that the Warrior cannot control your reactions, then you will have attained self-mastery. *Then* your peace will be full.'

'My students, the danger of any teacher and of any ashram is that it becomes an environment in which it is easy to maintain the appearance that everything is at peace. Everything here followed a certain formula where most of you rarely experienced something that disturbed your sense of having your lives under control.'

'I am not saying that you had not made progress. Most people in the world would not be able to live like you did. They have so much inner turbulence that they could not be at peace even in a peaceful environment. You had – through your diligent work and practice – risen to a stage where you did have the ability to be at peace in a peaceful environment.'

'I am not a Master who wants his students to go halfway on the path of self-mastery. I do not want you to have mastery only in ideal conditions. I want you to have mastery regardless of conditions; I want you to have unconditional mastery. For you to attain this higher mastery, you need to learn to maintain your inner peace even when faced with a person who has no peace and accuses you of all kinds of things that are not true.'

'I cannot teach you this because I am not willing to accuse you. The Warrior is therefore the teacher sent to all of us in order to test our inner resolve to go all the way to unconditional mastery over all conditions. As I have told you many times before, your primary concern should be whether you *reject* the test or *embrace* the test.'

The students look at each other, and the oldest says: 'Master, we see our limited vision, and we will strive to follow your directions. I see now that all of your teachings have been talking about this inner mastery, but I was not ready to acknowledge it until this moment.'

'My beloved students,' the Master says, 'when the student is ready, the teacher appears. The Warrior has appeared, which means you are ready for the test he represents. This also means you are capable of passing the test, for none are given a test until they are ready to pass it—*if* they transcend their present level of consciousness, *if* they let go of their present sense of self.'

'One last question, Master. You said that the Warrior is also being tested. What is *his* test?'

The Master answers: 'When I first met the Warrior years ago, he was ready for my teachings at the inner levels of his

1 | The Reluctant Student

being. As is so often the case, his outer mind or self was not ready to acknowledge this inner reality. Although he did recognize me as being a significant person, he was not willing to break off the track his life was on in order to learn from me.'

'This is the case for many people in this age. In the inner recesses of their beings, they are ready to walk the path of self-mastery. Their outer minds cannot accept this, partly because they have never been taught the path in a universal way. Such people need to enter the "School of Hard Knocks." It is only a matter of how hard the knocks have to become before they are ready to change course in life and acknowledge their inner desire to master their minds.'

'Most people have their minds locked on a track. They have a certain sense of who they are and how they are supposed to live their lives. Only when that outer, artificial identity is challenged, will the people be ready to acknowledge the inner path. For most people, only very hard blows can shatter the artificial identity and make them open to the inner path.'

'The Warrior has had the hard blows and his old identity is shattered. As so often happens, this has caused him to be psychologically wounded. The question now is whether we can help him come to the point of being willing to look beyond his wounds and acknowledge the innermost desire of his being. For us to be successful, we must show him something he has never met anywhere else. We must challenge the wounded identity he has built in order to deal with the loss of his artificial identity. We must help him see the potential for building a true identity from within.'

'So far, I have left him alone. We are now ready to take this to a new level by showing him more direct kindness. As a Master far greater than me taught, if you keep turning the other cheek, very few people can continue to strike you. Most will eventually be transformed by your kindness and stop responding with unkindness. Are you ready to enter this phase, my students?'

The students all nod, and one of them asks: 'Master, you said that not all people will be transformed if you turn the other cheek?'

'No, as the Great Master himself proved, some will indeed continue to attack you beyond all reason, even to the point of seeking to kill you, crucify you or destroy you psychologically. The Warrior is not in this category or I would not have invited him here. It is truly up to us to show him kindness to the point where he is either transformed or where he chooses to leave in order to avoid being transformed. We will leave that choice to him.'

2 | THE CENTRAL HUMAN DILEMMA

The Warrior asks the Master a question

More weeks pass and the students learn to transcend their reactions to the Warrior. As the Warrior senses a change in them, he stops being abusive. When he is successful in getting other people to react to his abuse, he feels a certain sense of power over them, and it alleviates his sense of being powerless. When he gets no reaction, his abuse no longer gives him a sense of power but only a sense of pointlessness. He feels even more powerless.

As the students learn not to react, the Master starts bringing the Warrior his evening meal. After putting the food on a small table, the Master walks to the door, turns around and looks directly at the Warrior for a few seconds.

For several weeks, the Warrior never looks back at the master but avoids his gaze. One day, the Warrior looks up, meets the Master's eyes and seems transfixed for several seconds. The Warrior finally looks down and says:

'I have been watching you, old man. You are the first person I have ever met who has had no reaction to me whatsoever. I have tried yelling at you, but I never sensed a reaction in you, as I did in your students for a time.'

'In the beginning, I thought you have no reaction because you don't care. But I have seen you look at me, and the only other place I have seen such an expression is in a woman looking at her newborn baby. Yet a baby is pure and innocent so *that* I can understand.'

'But look at me. I am a wreck of a man with a broken body and a broken mind. How can you look at me as if I was as innocent and pure as a baby?'

The Master looks at the Warrior for several seconds, then answers:

'When you look at yourself, you see only the body and the outer mind. I see beyond them. I see the self behind the outer clothing. No matter what has happened to you here on earth, that self is as pure and as innocent as when it was first created in the Crucible of Spirit.'

'When you are ready to look beyond the outer self and get to know who you really are, let me know and I will help you.'

Before the Warrior can speak, the Master is gone.

The Master asks the Warrior a question

More weeks pass. One day, the Master brings the Warrior his meal, stops in the doorway, looks at the Warrior and says: 'My Son, tell me about what you call the "Machine."'

The Warrior looks up with a surprised look, thinks for a few moments and says: 'When I was lying there in the desert, watching my blood soak into the sand, it was as if my eyes were opened. I saw what you said to me in the marketplace: Seeking to destroy someone else with anger can never bring peace.'

'I knew then that I had been fooled into going to war. I had been given an empty promise that by making a sacrifice for my country, I would help bring peace to the world. I saw that this promise was a sham, that it always *has been* a sham and that it always *will be* a sham.'

'I saw that reaching back into the mists of history, there has always been this force that has encouraged men to go to war. So many men have believed in the necessity of using violence to bring peace. So many have used this as an excuse to justify their destructive actions. So many have believed that even though they know in their hearts that force and violence is wrong, the evil of the enemy necessitates and justifies their own anger and their own use of force.'

'I saw in a flash that this is all a lie. I knew – I *experienced* – that violence and force are *never* justified, no matter what others do to you.'

'I then saw that there is an entire apparatus in the world, a kind of huge mind-control machine, that programs us to believe in this lie that the ends can justify the means. I saw how it is hiding behind the institutions of society, even the ideas that form the foundation for society. I saw how we are being programmed from childhood to accept the lie and to support the ongoing struggle created by the Machine.'

'I saw that the struggle is pointless, that it has no outcome. I saw that it will never bring peace nor any other positive goal. It will only support the survival and growth of the Machine. I knew then that my efforts had been in vain, and I felt the pointlessness and vanity of it all. I felt empty. *That* was when I gave up and just wanted to melt away into nothingness. I could see no purpose in continuing to live in order to support the Machine. I just wanted out of it. When I survived and was sent home, they attempted to offer me the usual help in getting back to civilian life. I saw that everything they did was controlled by the Machine and had the purpose of keeping me a slave of the Machine. The entire apparatus of sending soldiers to war and helping them come back is geared towards supporting the existence of the Machine. Even what we call "normal life" is controlled by the Machine. We claim to be living in a free country, but we are all enslaved by the Machine.'

'When I was lying there in the sand, I knew that the Machine does not care about anyone. The individual human being is completely insignificant to the Machine. It uses individuals to further its ends, and when they have nothing more to offer, it wants them to be silent or be so trapped in suffering that they cannot challenge its control over the population.'

'I decided that I wanted nothing more to do with the Machine, neither in war nor in what was supposed to be normal life. I rebelled against their attempts to reintegrate me into society, for I no longer wanted to be part of a society run by the Machine. I rebelled against everything, and that is why I ended up on the street. But at least I was on my own and no longer controlled by the Machine.'

Submission versus rebellion

The Master looks at the Warrior for several seconds, then asks: 'My Son, have you ever considered that whether you *submit* to the Machine or *rebel* against the Machine, your life is still controlled by the Machine?'

The Warrior looks up with a stunned expression. His mind is racing, but in order to buy time, he asks: 'What do you mean? Surely, when I was in the army, my life was controlled by the

2 | The Central Human Dilemma

Machine, but since then I have rebelled against everything the Machine wants me to do so it can no longer control me as it used to do.'

The Master replies: 'How does the Machine control you? Where is the mechanism that allows it to control you?'

The Warrior says: 'The Machine controls society and as long as I am part of society, it can control me. I had to withdraw from society in order to escape its control. I am rebelling against everything the Machine stands for in order to avoid submitting to it.'

The Master says: 'My Son, you have had important insights about the existence of the Machine and how it seeks to control us all. Yet I am asking you to consider whether there might not be an insight that has eluded you.'

'After all, you said yourself that it is a mind-control machine. It controls you by controlling your *mind*. The mechanism that controls you is not "out there" but "in here," inside your own mind. It is here you must win your freedom from the Machine. What you saw in the desert was that fighting an external enemy will not bring peace to the world. What you have not yet seen is that fighting an enemy in the mind will not bring you inner peace.'

'It is true that submitting to the Machine will allow it to control you. Yet rebelling against the Machine will also allow it to control you. Whether you do what the Machine tells you to do or whether you do the opposite of what the Machine tells you to do, your thinking is still affected by the Machine. Those who rebel are no more free than those who submit.'

'True inner peace, true mastery of self, comes when you transcend the consciousness behind the Machine, when you find the Middle Way beyond submission and rebellion. Your reactions to life are neither submissive to nor rebellious against the Machine. You are free when you can live your life in this world without being affected in any way by the Machine that thinks it owns this world. You are free from the Machine only when it becomes irrelevant to you.'

'My Son, I have seen from the start that at inner levels of your being, you are ready to engage the path to this form of self-mastery. I invited you here as an offer to help you. Are you ready to accept my assistance or do you need more time to experience what it is like to have your mind controlled by the Machine?'

'Let me know when you have an answer to this question.'

The Warrior attempts to leave

One morning the Master is sitting in his room in deep meditation. The oldest student knocks on the door, sticks his head in and says: 'Master, the Warrior is packing up his things and he says he is going to leave. You told me to tell you if this happened.'

The Master opens one eye and says: 'Ask him this: "Why are you so afraid of being free that you have to run away from the man who holds the key to your freedom?"'

The student leaves and the Master continues his meditation. When the Master is done and leaves his room for breakfast, he finds the Warrior sitting in his wheelchair outside the door. The Warrior says: 'Old man, I think I am ready for you to help me.'

The Master looks at him with a penetrating gaze and says: 'I know you are ready at inner levels, but I still see that your outer mind is trapped in rebellion. I do not "help" people. I take on students who are ready for the kind of teaching I provide. That means a student must willingly submit himself to whatever I require of him.'

'If you are willing to apply yourself as any other student of mine, then I can help you. If you want me to help you on *your* terms, it would be a waste of time for both of us. What is your true desire?'

The Warrior looks stunned, thinks for some time and says: 'Okay, Master, I am willing to submit to your teaching methods.'

The Master says: 'Then I accept you as a student. Here is your first assignment. Take a shower and comb or cut your hair and beard. Put on some new clothes that my other students will give you. Then meet me in the assembly hall after breakfast.'

The Master's first instructions to the Warrior

The Warrior sits among the students in the ashrams' assembly hall. His hair is cut to normal length and his beard trimmed short. He is wearing comfortable clothes like the other students. The Master is sitting in the circle without standing out from the students.

They are all sitting on low chair pads with a backrest and thick foam padding. The chairs are comfortable for meditating or listening to teachings for a long period of time. The hall has white walls and ceiling and a thick white carpet. It has rounded corners so nothing attracts attention. There is no altar or any form of decoration. One wall is made entirely of glass and gives a view of a thicket of large pine trees outside. A squirrel is busy gathering pine cones.

The students have just finished a lengthy session of performing spiritual exercises in the form of spoken invocations. The Master makes a short invocation, calling for beings of light to join them. He then has the students recite the OM several times, each time drawing it out longer. He finally looks at the Warrior and says: 'We all welcome you to our circle of oneness. We accept you as one of us, as in every way worthy and equal with us.'

The students all look at the Warrior, who first seems uncomfortable, but then surrenders and looks each of the students in the eye. When he reaches the Master, his eyes are filled with tears.

The Master says: 'In this lifetime, I am playing the role of the teacher. There are many teachers in the world. None of us have a patent on truth or the highest possible teaching. We each have an individual teaching that it is our role to teach. I can only teach the teaching I have received and internalized. This is my assignment and my joy.'

'As my student, it is your task to absorb my teaching and allow it to change you. If you find that the teaching does not have what you need or that you need something else, you are always free to move on to another teacher. When I say *my* student I do not in any way claim ownership of you.'

'When I talk about *my* teaching, I also claim no ownership. We do not have ownership of anything in this world. If we claim ownership, what we claim to own ends up owning us. I only use the expression *my* teaching for practical purposes, as a figure of speech.'

'What I teach is how to attain peace of mind by learning how the mind works and then using that knowledge to be in command of your thoughts and feelings. What you call the Machine, and which I call the collective beast or spirit, seeks to control you by taking away your peace of mind. It seeks to get you into an agitated state of mind where you are struggling against something.'

'The Machine seeks to control you by getting you to react against something. The sole purpose is that this struggle feeds your psychic energy to the Machine, which is what the beast requires in order to survive and grow in power. Any reaction – *any* reaction – is an inroad for the Machine to control your mind.'

'This collective spirit has been created by humankind over a very long period of time. Innumerable are the schemes that have been defined in order to keep people trapped in the struggle. Each person has come to accept some of the ideas and beliefs that seemingly justify these schemes. It is these beliefs that keep you trapped in the struggle. In order to be free, you need to unravel them one by one. This cannot be done in a short period of time, for the beliefs have become part of your sense of identity.'

The energy equation

'In order to begin the process, you must come to understand that what takes away your inner peace is a combination of beliefs and energy. You live in a world where everything is energy. Energy has different levels of vibration. Physical matter is made from energies that vibrate within a certain spectrum. Your senses are calibrated to detect these energies as a solid substance that people normally call "matter."'

'There are energies that have much higher vibrations than the level of matter. Some of them are what I call psychic energy, meaning energies that drive your thoughts and feelings. Your physical senses cannot detect these energies, but many people have developed an ability to intuitively sense psychic energies. One can develop the ability to see these energies and even higher energies. Science is on the brink of developing mechanical devices that can show some of these energies. There is nothing hidden that shall not be revealed.'

'Your mind can be conscious and form thoughts and feelings only because it has a stream of psychic energy flowing through it. As the energy flows through your mind, it is changed in vibration by your beliefs. Some of the energy you generate will accumulate in the subconscious parts of the mind. When the accumulation reaches a certain point, it will form a psychic magnet that pulls your conscious mind into repeating certain patterns. This qualifies more energy and quickly becomes a self-reinforcing spiral that takes over your life. You become like a cow who is milked for energy that is then fed to the individual and collective spirits. No one can attain inner peace without breaking these patterns.'

'Do you, my Son, recognize how your life has been influenced by the energy in your own mind, or energy field?'

The Warrior answers: 'I am not sure; can you help me see this?"

The Master answers: "Think back to when I first met you. You were determined to destroy the enemy. Your mind was completely closed to any alternative. The closing of your mind was a result of the fact that anger energy had accumulated in your energy field. This anger was the magnet that pulled your mind into being completely focused on fighting the enemy, making it closed to a different approach to life.'

'Do you see how the anger compelled you into joining the army and how it kept accumulating as you became the "perfect killing machine?" Do you see that after you were wounded, the anger became even more intense to the point where you rejected all help? You were sitting on the street so controlled by the anger that you were shouting profanities at everyone.'

"Master, I do see this.' the Warrior answers, 'I just never saw how I was controlled by the anger.'

'Yes,' the Master says, 'when these psychic energies accumulate, they completely take over our minds. That is how the

Machine controls you. Through your anger, or any other fear-based emotion, you feed your psychic energy to the collective spirit. This also opens your mind to an inflow of chaotic energy from the Machine, and this energy overwhelms or takes over your individual mind. The energies are so intense that they form a veil that blinds you. You can see no alternative to continuing the pattern endlessly. Are you still determined to free yourself from the control of the Machine?'

'Yes, Master, I am.'

'Then my first task for you is to enter an intensive program of performing a set of special exercises along with my other students. They will help you clear your energy field of this downward spiral of anger energy. Only when the chaotic energy has been cleared, can I help you see the underlying beliefs that started the downward spiral. Only when the water of your mind becomes still, will you be able to look into the depth of the subconscious.'

'The way to free yourself from a downward energetic spiral is simple. Energy is a wave. If lower energy, such as anger, is met with a higher, love-based energy wave, the lower energy will be raised in vibration. My students will teach you a method for using the spoken word for invoking love-based energy. When you have cleared a critical mass of the anger energy, I will help you see the beliefs that launched your downward slide.'

The Warrior's anger against God

Weeks pass. The other students take the Warrior under their wings and help him learn the techniques for transforming anger energy. At first, the Warrior is reluctant, but he soon notices that he starts feeling more free and calm. He then becomes an eager practitioner. The Warrior also participates in the sessions where the Master teaches. One day, during such a session, the Master looks at the Warrior and says:

'I see that you have transformed a sufficient amount of anger energy that we can take the next step. You told me a long time ago that when you were lying wounded in the sand, you felt anger towards everything, even God and life. Have you ever considered why we human beings can feel anger towards life or God?'

'No, I never thought about that,' answers the Warrior.

The Master says: 'Close your eyes and mentally project yourself back to the situation in the desert. Describe the situation for me as if you are experiencing it in the present moment.'

The Warrior begins hesitantly: 'I heard this overwhelmingly loud blast that stunned my senses. I am just coming back to some sense of consciousness.'

'I feel no pain, but then I look down at my one leg. I see that the foot and the lower leg are just a lump of bloody meat. I even see bone fragments sticking out of the blood. I see my blood seeping into the yellow sand. I raise my eyes and look towards the horizon.'

'Now describe what is going on in your mind,' says the Master.

'As I look at my leg, I first feel disbelief. But then it hits me with a force that almost makes me throw up: *This is real!* This has really happened! My leg is shattered and *nothing* can change this fact. I am going to bleed to death here in this remote desert.'

'My mind is then flooded with questions. How could this happen? How could this happen to *me?* I am supposed to be the invincible warrior. A minute ago I *was* indeed the invincible warrior but now I am reduced to a helpless wreck.'

2 | The Central Human Dilemma

'It is as if I go out of my body. I am outside time and space. I start seeing this vision of the Machine while the events of my life flash before my inner eye.'

'After the vision fades, I am again back in my body, and now I start to feel this deep inner rage. I am angry at the enemy for planting this cowardly bomb. But first of all, I am angry at God for letting this happen. When I joined the army, I thought I was on God's side, that I was fighting for peace, that I was doing what God wanted. I now experience that this is all a sham created by the Machine.'

'I see that God never wanted us to fight and kill each other in his name or for a cause that we think is his but that only serves to uphold the Machine. I see that it is never justified by God that we kill or force other human beings.'

'My mind now begins to spin and it says that God has created me and everything. God has created the world and allowed us humans to create our own hell on earth. So God has given me the life that got me in this situation where I am facing consequences that can never be undone. I cannot undo the damage done to my physical body. How can I ever undo the damage done to my soul as a result of experiencing such harsh consequences?'

The Master says: 'Good, very good. I know this situation is very painful for you so I am asking you to recite the OM with all of us.'

The Master, the Warrior and the other students recite the OM many times. The Master then says: 'I now ask you to consider that you have just relived the situation for the first time. Do you recognize that even though the situation has intruded itself upon your awareness many times, you have never before been able to actually go into it and relive it?'

'Yes, I can see that,' the Warrior says with a surprised expression.

The Master continues: 'The reason is that you have spent weeks practicing the techniques for transforming energy. When we experience a traumatic situation, a huge amount of fear-based energy is generated. More energy is added as we deal with the consequences of the situation. This energy is stored in the subconscious mind, and it causes us pain when the conscious mind touches it. This explains why reliving the situation would be far too painful to endure, which is why we tend to suppress it if at all possible. We go into various forms of denial in order to avoid the pain that would overwhelm us.'

'You have now transformed so much of the energy that you were able to actually relive the situation. Although you still feel a lot of negative energy, this is a significant victory for you. I realize you may not see it that way, but do you think you are ready to talk about the situation or do you feel you need time to rest or process the feeling?'

'No,' the Warrior answers, 'I think I am ready to talk.'

The Master says: 'Good. What you experienced in that situation is the very core of what it means to be a human being in a world where matter is so dense that certain consequences cannot be physically undone. The very essence of human existence is that we find ourselves in a world that forces us to make choices.'

'All of our choices have consequences. Once the choice is made and the consequence has become a physical circumstance, it is either impossible or very difficult to undo the consequence. We now have to deal with the consequences of previous choices. This forces us to make new choices that create other consequences. This becomes a merry-go-round that keeps us trapped in what seems like endless suffering.'

'Given the current state of the collective consciousness, most human beings resent being in this situation. They resent being forced to make choices and then having to face the consequences of their choices. They often feel that they are forced by circumstances to make a choice, that they have only one choice and that therefore they could not have avoided the unpleasant consequences they now face.'

'Those who believe in God must reason that God has put them in this situation. The inevitable result is that they resent God and feel a deep anger against God. Many people do not recognize this anger because they have covered it over with an outer persona based on their particular religion. They feel it is wrong to be angry with God so they direct their anger towards other people or a devil who supposedly threatens God's plan and power. This is not constructive because *all* of your anger stems from the core anger against God.'

'People who do not believe in God must reason that life or other people force them to make choices and face the consequences. They direct their anger against "life" but more often against other people.'

'Whether they believe in God or not, most people seek to deal with their anger by engaging in the primary pastime on earth, namely the attempt to change your own state of mind by changing other people. You attempt to change what is going on *inside* your mind by seeking to change what is going on *outside* your mind. It is this very struggle that keeps the Machine alive.'

How the Machine controls people

The Master continues: "My Son, you have seen that there is a machine or spirit that attempts to control the world. I am now asking you to consider how the Machine can control you as an individual being. In order to help you see this, I ask you to consider what kind of being you actually are. I am not asking *who* you are but *what* you are?'

The Warrior ponders this, but ends up with a puzzled look on his face. 'Help me along, I cannot see what you want me to consider.'

The Master answers: 'When you were lying there in the sand, you experienced that a part of you went outside your physical body. You had the direct experience that there is a part of your mind that can actually be conscious and that can experience life without doing so through the senses or brain of the physical body.'

'If you think more deeply about this, you will realize that there is a part of you that experienced life without doing so through the filter of your outer mind, your normal state of consciousness. You were a neutral observer, a silent witness. Do you recognize this?'

'I never thought about it before, but yes, I do see that.'

'Then what does this mean in terms of what you are, what kind of being you are?'

The Warrior thinks for some time, then says: 'I guess it means that I am not my physical body. I am more than the body. But wait, I also experienced that I am more than the outer mind and personality. So that must mean I'm not actually a physical, material being. I am a mind. The core of my being is a mind, a form of consciousness. This mind is not my outer mind but something deeper.'

'I guess it is even timeless because I experienced a state of mind that was beyond time and space, yet it felt completely real. It actually felt *more real* than what I normally experience. So I am mind, I am a form of consciousness or self that is beyond time and space.'

The Master says: 'Very good. You have now become aware of the one foundational realization that can take you out of the

2 | The Central Human Dilemma

common human struggle and take you further on the path of self-mastery. This is the master key to escaping the Machine.'

'The central human dilemma is that we find ourselves in a world that forces us to make choices and that we cannot escape the physical consequences of those choices. We are trapped in a seemingly never-ending cycle of facing circumstances that limit our options yet force us to make a choice. Our choices create consequences and we are then forced to make further choices based on the consequences of our previous choices. It seems like we can never get off the treadmill.'

'The very first step towards breaking this cycle is the realization you have just had, namely that you are not a material being but a non-material mind. Once you realize this, you begin to see that if you are not a material being, you do not need to be bound by material conditions or the material consequences of your own choices.'

'The very foundation – the *only* foundation – for reaching this conclusion is that you must have a direct experience of a state of consciousness that is not dependent on the physical body and outer mind.'

'In your case, you had this mystical or transcendental experience as a result of a very dramatic physical situation. Many people do indeed need to have certain physical experiences and face certain physical consequences before they are able to step outside the body and the outer mind. This is what I call the School of Hard Knocks.'

'Some people are able to have such experiences as a result of studying spiritual teachings and practicing spiritual techniques. If you use the techniques I have taught you for transforming fear-based energy, you will spontaneously have such experiences. Some people have had transcendental experiences without deliberately, at least not consciously, doing anything to achieve them.'

'Most people either have not had such experiences or they have not consciously acknowledged them. For such people my words would only seem like another round of psychobabble and they might argue against them. Such people I cannot help. They must take another round in the School of Hard Knocks until they face physical consequences so shocking that they finally go outside their human selves and experience their timeless selves.'

'Since you have had a transcendental experience and since you have now started to realize what the experience means, we can take the next step. I now ask that every day you continue to practice the techniques for transforming energy. After you are done with one session, you spend some time contemplating the question: "What am I?"'

'What you do is that you ask yourself a series of questions. You can start by asking: "Am I the tree outside my window?"'

'The answer is obviously a "No," and you then ask: "Am I this building?" "Am I the mountain?" "Am I this physical body?"'

'When you realize you are not the body, you can ask further questions about your outer mind. You can go into your feelings and ask whether you are a particular feeling, whether you are a particular thought or even a particular sense of self. *Then* tune in to your anger and ask yourself: "Am I the anger or am I more than the anger?"'

'I realize you already have an intellectual understanding that you are not the body and the outer mind. There is still value in going through this exercise every day for some time. Intellectual knowledge never changes anyone's consciousness. Only a direct inner experience, an Aha experience, can shift your consciousness.'

3 | THE WARRIOR DISCOVERS HIS LIFE GOAL

A couple of weeks pass. One day, as the students are sitting in the assembly hall, the Master looks at the Warrior and says: 'You have practiced the technique of asking "Am I this, am I that." Describe to me what you experienced.'

The Warrior answers: 'At first, I got nowhere with the meditation. I felt kind of stupid for asking these questions because, as you said, I intellectually knew the answer. So for several days I became increasingly irritated and even angry at you for having me do this exercise.'

'One day, something happened. I suddenly saw in a flash that what I was doing in rebelling against the exercise was the same I had been doing after returning from war. I saw that I was letting my anger build up. I literally saw for my inner eye how there was this maelstrom of anger energy inside my own mind. I saw how my attention was being magnetically drawn into it and how this took away my awareness of anything else.'

'I now focused on the maelstrom of energy. In a flash I saw how my personal energy spiral was tied in to this huge collective maelstrom of anger energy that is bigger than the planet. I looked into this black hole of swirling energy and it scared the hell out of me because I felt how, as an individual, I was completely powerless to resist this pull. I saw how this anger energy upholds the Machine and how the Machine can control everybody by pulling their attention into thinking they have to engage life with anger.'

'At first, I was so scared that I didn't know what to do. For several days I couldn't even meditate, but I then used the techniques for transforming energy to deal with the anger spiral in my own mind. After some time, I again tried the meditation, and now I felt how I no longer resisted it.'

'One day, as I was going through the steps of "I am not this, I am not that," I suddenly felt like I went outside my body and I had the same experience as I had in the desert, but this time it was different—or perhaps I saw it differently. Back then, I was in a situation where I faced this very harsh consequence so I did not realize that when I was outside of my body I felt at peace. This time, I felt that peace and it was really special. It was the first time in my life where I felt my mind and emotions were calm. It was like looking at the sea in the early morning when it is calm as a mirror.'

'I then experienced how I simply looked at the anger spiral and its tie to the planetary spiral, and I experienced that the bigger spiral has no power over me when I am centered in this peace. I knew that the Machine can only control me by getting me to react in some way. When I don't react, it is as if I am untouchable to the Machine.'

'Of course, as soon as I went out of the experience, I was back in my old frame of mind and I found myself reacting again. Yet I am very excited because now I have experienced that it is possible for me to get away from being controlled by the Machine. I have experienced the reality of your words that whether I comply with the Machine or rebel against it, I am still controlled by the Machine. I now see that I really, really want you to help me stop reacting to the Machine. This is my new life goal, and I haven't had a life goal for a long time.'

Breaking out of the human treadmill

The Master says: 'My Son, you are bringing tears of joy to an old man's eyes. Do you now see why I had you spend so much time on these practical exercises? No amount of theoretical knowledge and intellectual understanding will give you what you have now had: a direct experience that you are more than your psychical body and outer mind. You are more than your feelings and thoughts. Your are more than the energy maelstrom in your personal field.'

'Unless you have that experience, giving you teachings will get you nowhere. In fact, it might take you further from the goal by making you prideful that you know so much.'

'The dilemma for a spiritual teacher is that while the student needs a direct experience that he or she is more than the psychic energies, these very energies pull on the student's attention and prevent him or her from having the experience of stepping outside the energies. We had to break that spiral and you have done so. We can now take the next step.'

'I now ask you to consider what I said earlier about the central human dilemma. I said that we find ourselves in a world where circumstances force us to make choices. Our choices have consequences and when we experience those consequences, we feel forced to make new choices. Based on what you have experienced, can you begin to see how we can break that spiral of feeling increasingly forced, feeling like we have fewer and fewer options, like we have only one choice?'

The Warrior thinks for some time, then says: 'I assume you mean that when I experience that I am not the outer mind, I can look at my situation without reacting to it through the outer mind?'

The Master says: 'Exactly! You have seen how the Machine pulls on people's attention. It pulls their conscious attention into looking at life and every situation in life through a filter, a perception filter, made up of the outer mind and personality.'

'Take any situation you encounter in life. You look at the situation through your perception filter, and then you react to the situation through that same filter. The perception filter limits the options you can see. There may be a dozen ways to react to a given situation but because of your filter, you can see only two, perhaps only one.'

'Each of the dozen ways to react would create a different consequence, some more pleasant than others. When you are trapped in a spiral of negative feelings, you can see only the option that creates the most unpleasant consequences. You feel forced to choose what seems like your only option. This creates a consequence. As you are faced with the consequence, you look at it through the same perception filter that caused you to create the consequence in the first place.'

'Because your perception filter enabled you to see only one option, you felt forced to do what you did by external circumstances. You now blame the external circumstances for the consequences and since you cannot see how to escape those consequences, you feel powerless to change your life. Again, you can see only one option, namely to respond with the same negative feelings that caused you to make the previous choice. This takes you further and further into frustration and anger. You are in a downward spiral and you feel powerless to stop it.'

3 | The Warrior Discovers His Life Goal

'Take your own life. If you look back, you will see how, in early childhood, you began building your personal spiral of anger energy. In your case, you did this by reacting to your father's anger. He had built his spiral by reacting to his own father's anger, and so on for generations. Your spiral became stronger and stronger, and you started taking it out on other people. You will see how you took your anger out on your siblings, your parents, your teachers and your supervisors at work.'

'When your nation was attacked, your own anger compelled you to respond by joining the army. In your outer mind, you thought you were responding to the call of defending your nation and even fighting for God's cause. The deeper reality was that you made the choice you made because your anger spiral had taken such control of your life that you needed an ultimate enemy as the target for your anger. Going into a physical war was the ultimate way for you to take your own internal anger energy out on other people.'

'I know this is a brutal way of putting it so what do you feel about what I am saying?'

When the cause is outside ourselves

The Warrior answers: 'No, no, it's not too brutal; it's very accurate. I now see that this is exactly what I was doing. My whole life and my outlook on life was controlled by this spiral of anger energy.'

The Master says: 'Good, then we can go one step further. When we are trapped in such a spiral of negative energy – and I have been there myself – we look at life from inside the cloud of energy, from inside the perception filter, and what do we see? We see life from the most negative possible outlook, we have a deficit approach to life. When a certain outer situation comes up, we see only two options: Is it what we want or is it not what we want? If it *is* what we want, we do not feel threatened but we are not actually happy and at peace about it either. We are on guard for the next situation that is not what we want. If a situation *is not* what we want, then we can see only one way to react, namely with anger—or whatever energy makes up our personal spiral.'

'In your case, you built a personal spiral of anger, and it colored the way you looked at every situation. When a situation was not what you wanted, you could see no other way to react than with anger, and you felt the anger was perfectly justified. Do you see this?'

'Yes, Master, I see this.'

'Good, then go one step further. In your vision, the anger was the only way to react and it was perfectly justified because of what the outer situation was presenting to you. Where did you perceive that the cause of the anger was located? What caused the anger?'

The Warrior looks like he has had an epiphany and says excitedly: 'Oh, I see this. I saw the cause of the anger as being outside myself, I always thought that it was the other people that caused my anger, that it was the world that caused the anger.'

'Yes,' says the Master, 'and what does that mean for your ability to deliberately and consciously change your life?'

The Warrior continues excitedly: 'I see this now. The anger was actually inside *me*. The cause of the anger was inside me. Yet when I projected that the cause was outside myself, I also gave away my power to do anything about the cause. I actually gave away my power to control my own destiny. I gave that power to the anger in myself and to the collective spiral of anger outside myself. I gave my power to the Machine!'

3 | *The Warrior Discovers His Life Goal*

The Warrior says, with tears in his eyes: 'Master, I want to be free from this entire downward spiral—I just want to be free.'

The Master answers with great love: 'And you will be, if you continue to build on the experiences and insights you have now had.'

Cause, effect and consciousness

'You now see the central human dilemma in a new light. We make a choice based on a certain state of consciousness. The choice is limited because our own beliefs and energy spirals limit the options we can see. As a result, we choose the option with the most unpleasant consequences—which we do not realize until later. When we are faced with those consequences, we look at them through the same perception filter that caused us to make the previous choice.'

'We now react with the same fear-based outlook and make a choice that only takes us further down the same path. We have created a downward spiral and our own perception filter and choices make it a self-reinforcing spiral.'

'In your case, each situation caused an angry reaction. You responded to the situation from that consciousness of anger. Each such choice led to an outcome that only made you more angry. This kept building throughout your life, giving away your power to choose a non-angry reaction.'

'We cannot take back our power to change our lives until we see that we are in a downward spiral and consciously make a choice that is *not* colored by the perception filter that created the spiral. Such a life choice can only come from an inner epiphany, an intuitive breakthrough, an Aha experience. The question now becomes what can bring about this inner shift.'

'For some people the shift can happen only as a result of a very shocking experience. Some have to follow their personal downward spiral until they feel they hit bottom and can go no further. *Then* the shift occurs. They now start moving up by realizing that they are the ones who have to change and that the change begins in the mind with their attitude and outlook on life. Others can get an inner epiphany by observing other people or through a teaching that deals with these issues. Regardless of how you arrive at the shift, all that matters is that you now see an alternative to continuing in your personal downward spiral. My Son, do you see that alternative?'

The Warrior again thinks carefully, then says: 'I assume you mean that I can learn to react to a situation in a way that is not predetermined by what you call my perception filter? I can learn to step outside my angry personality and look at a situation the way I do when I go outside my body?'

The Master says: 'You are correct. When we look at any situation from inside the perception filter, we think it is the external situation that causes our reaction to it. Therefore, the choice we make is predetermined. "I had no other choice" as people so often say. The reason you had no other choice was that your internal perception filter prevented you from seeing any other options.'

'In reality, the cause of our reaction is our own internal conditions. The outer situation can only trigger the cause that is already inside our minds. Science has taught us the concept of action and reaction. A certain action will mechanically lead to a certain reaction. If you throw a rock up into the air, the force of gravity will automatically cause it to fall down.'

'When we human beings allow our vision of life to be colored by an internal perception filter, we become mechanical beings, we become robots. This is exactly how the Machine controls us.'

'It first presents us with unpleasant outer circumstances, for example by having other people force us, and over time we build a perception filter. This filter is based on a set of non-constructive beliefs about what the world is like, combined with a spiral of fear-based energy. The combination of beliefs and energy prevents us from seeing more than one or a few options for responding to a given situation. No matter what option we choose, it leads to consequences that reinforce our world view and reinforce the negative energy spiral.'

'The most subtle effect of the Machine is that it turns us into mechanical beings. Our beliefs and the energy spirals draw our conscious attention away from the recognition that we are creative beings. When I say "creative beings," I mean that we have the potential to make creative, rather than mechanical, choices about how we respond to a given situation. As you have experienced yourself, you are more than the outer personality with its beliefs and energy spirals.'

'When you first came here, you had such an intense spiral of anger energy that it pulled your conscious mind into fully identifying with the outer personality. Because you have been so diligent in practicing the techniques for transforming some of the energy in the spiral, you are now able to avoid being pulled into the outer personality. You can use your mind's natural ability to project itself anywhere it wants, including outside your normal perception filter.'

'You can step outside your perception filter and look at the situation as a neutral witness. You can break the cause-effect pattern where your outer personality determines your reactions by filtering out all but one option. You can take back your power to make a creative choice so that you do not react to a situation through your outer personality. You can make a creative choice only when you see more than one option. You are free to consciously choose a different reaction than the one dictated by your perception filter. You are free to make a new choice independently of your past choices. You are free to make a *real* choice. Doing this and doing this consciously is the very key – the *only* key – to breaking out of the human dilemma.'

4 | SEEING THE "ENEMY" WITHIN

The high-wire exercise

The Master says: 'You have made excellent progress. What I want you to do next is to continue to practice the techniques for transforming fear-based energy. There is still much energy accumulated in the subconscious layers of your mind, and we need to continue to reduce its magnetic pull on your conscious mind.'

'After each time you have invoked energy, I want you to sit quietly and imagine that you are in a circus. You are standing on a high tower and in front of you is a wire leading towards another tower on the opposite side of the circus ring. There is, of course, a safety net and you have both of your legs in perfect working order.'

'You now visualize that the circus tent itself acts as a protective cage that seals you from all lower energies coming from the outside world. You have already learned to invoke spiritual protection that seals your mind from the energy spirals that make up the Machine.'

'You visualize that you are sealed from all outside pulls. There is nothing pulling on you except what is happening inside your own mind. You now visualize that you start walking out on the wire. The only way to keep your balance and avoid falling into the safety net below is to keep your mind neutral, to keep it clear from anything that pulls you towards one side or the other.'

'As you visualize walking out on the wire, you watch your mind and see how long you can keep it neutral. It may be that thoughts, feelings or sensations come up that take your attention away from the exercise. When this happens, you might be caught up in the thoughts for some time, but eventually you will become aware that you have shifted your attention away from the exercise. This will mean that you have been pulled off balance and you will have fallen off the wire and into the safety net below.'

'I now want you to visualize that you climb down from the safety net, walk over to the ladder and climb it step by step until you are back on the platform. I want there to be a "penalty" in the form of some mental labor involved after you fall off the wire. Once you are back on the platform, you again seek inner balance and walk out on the wire, seeing how long you can keep your mind in neutral. When you again fall into thoughts, you repeat the process.'

'In the beginning, do not practice this exercise for too long. If you feel that it becomes a source of stress, simply stop and wait until the next time you have invoked energy.'

'After you practice the exercise for some time and feel comfortable with it, I want you to start paying attention to what is pulling you out of balance. You will notice that it is the same kind of feelings or thoughts that come up again and again. I then want you to use the techniques for invoking energy to transform the kind of energies that you are dealing with. After you have done this for some time, we will talk again.'

Why the struggle goes on indefinitely

After some time, the Master asks the Warrior how he has experienced the high-wire exercise and he replies: 'I am sure glad you told me not to practice it too much because it caused me a lot of stress in the beginning. I first had trouble even imagining that I have two normal legs and can actually walk a high-wire. I could not even imagine having my leg back. I worked on this for days by invoking the violet flame energy as the other students have taught me.'

'I realized the problem was that there was a lot of anger energy related to my losing my leg and it was pulling my mind out of balance before I could even imagine stepping onto the wire.'

'It took me an amazingly long time to get over this, but eventually the energy was so dissipated that I could imagine stepping onto the wire. Yet I would barely get on to it before my mind was pulled into thinking about me losing my leg so I have not taken more than a couple of steps onto the wire before falling off.'

The Master says: 'This is a good result. What is the pattern you have uncovered that pulls your mind out of balance?'

'It is losing my leg, of course,' the Warrior replies. "I just can't seem to stop thinking about that and what it felt like when I realized nothing could ever make this undone.'

'That is very understandable,' the Master says, 'but perhaps we can eventually help you see that consequences can indeed be undone, although not the way most people think. What I want you to do now is describe the feeling you have with one word.'

The Warrior thinks for a moment, then says: 'Guilt. I feel guilty for making the stupid choices that led me to go to war and have my leg blown off.'

'Good, very good' the Master says.

'Why is that good?' the Warrior says with a hint of his old anger. 'I just feel lousy for having been stupid enough to make those kind of choices that I can never undo. What could be good about that?'

The Master replies with disarming calm: 'It is good because it demonstrates that you have taken an important step on your journey of freeing yourself from the clutches of the Machine. Think back to what you told me when we met in the marketplace before you came here. Do you remember telling me that when you were lying there in the sand, looking at your wounded leg, you felt anger towards the enemy, luck, life and God?'

'Well, yes, I do remember that.'

'Then, can you not see that what you just told me shows that you have already moved to a higher state of consciousness, you have already started to free yourself from your previous perception filter?'

The Warrior looks perplexed so the Master continues: 'Before you came here, your attention and your anger was completely directed outwards. The cause of your misery was the enemy, the Machine, life, luck or God. What was missing from the picture, what was the factor that you did not consider?'

'Oh, I see,' says the Warrior, 'you mean I was not considering myself. I was projecting that the cause was "out there" and that I had nothing to do with it?'

4 | Seeing the "Enemy" Within

'Exactly, and based on the insight you had some time ago, what had you actually done to yourself by projecting the cause away from yourself?'

The Warrior says: 'You mean that by projecting that the cause was outside myself, I had given away my power to do anything about my situation. I had disempowered myself?'

The Master nods and the Warrior continues: 'Of course, you are right. If God or life is responsible for my situation, it follows that the only way to change my situation is to find some way to control God or life. Since that is impossible, I am stuck in my misery and there is nothing I can do about it.'

The Master says: 'What does that make you feel like?'

'I feel powerless!' The Warrior replies.

The Master says: 'Yes, and if you look at most people on this planet, they have a deep, often unrecognized, sense of being powerless, of having no way to change their life experience. They engage in all kinds of compensatory behavior aimed at giving them some fleeting sense of not being powerless because there is something they can control. If you look closely at this, you see that they feel powerless because they think their experience of life on this planet depends on factors over which they have little or no control, such as life, luck, fate or God.'

'If you go even deeper, you see that the real issue is a belief that the way you experience life on this planet depends on material conditions. Most conditions people cannot change. As a result they feel powerless. The history of humankind can be seen as a way for people to overcome the sense of being powerless by finding some way to control the material conditions they face on this planet. Technology and knowledge have allowed people to make some progress in controlling certain conditions. Yet there is one condition that it is still difficult for most people to control, and that is other people. The history of humankind can be seen as a process of people seeking to control each other. This is the primary mechanism that allows the Machine to perpetuate the ongoing human struggle.'

'What is the mechanism behind this struggle, what created it in the first place? It is the illusion that the only way for you to gain control over your experience of life is to change something or someone *outside* yourself.'

'Where does your experience of life take place? It takes place *inside* yourself, inside your mind. As you have seen yourself, you are not a material being; you are a mind. A mind can be seen as an experience device; it is something that experiences. What really matters in life is not the material conditions you face but your inner experience of those conditions, your life experience.'

'The Machine programs you to think that the only way to improve your life experience is to change your material circumstances, including other people. Is it logical to assume that the only, or the best, way to control an *inner* experience is to seek to control something *outside* yourself, something over which you obviously have little or no direct control? My Son, do you see that as long as you allow yourself to believe that your internal experience is the exclusive product of external conditions, you will remain powerless indefinitely?'

The Warrior answers with great enthusiasm: 'Master, you have opened my eyes. As you were speaking, I went out of my body and outer mind, and I saw how the Machine controls people through this belief that we must control what is outside ourselves. I saw how this has created and perpetuates the struggle. If I think I have to control other people, I will always be in a struggle against them. It can be no other way.'

'Yet, Master, I still feel guilt over making the choice to go to war so how do I deal with guilt?'

Guilt as a necessary phase

The Master says: 'My Son, you have seen the reality that most people are powerless because they think they have to seek control over that which they cannot control. You have seen how this has created the struggle and how it can perpetuate the struggle indefinitely. The struggle literally becomes a closed system from which there is no way out. The more you struggle, the more it seems you have to struggle.'

'The psychology of the situation is that you think external conditions are the cause of your state of mind. Your inner experience is the way it is because external conditions are the way they are. Only if external conditions change, will your state of mind change.'

'When you step back, you see that behind this is the belief that you have no power over your reaction to external conditions. You have only one way to react, meaning that you have no choice in the matter. Outer conditions force you to make a certain choice, and you have only one possible reaction to the consequences of your choice. Both the choice and your reaction to the consequences are forced upon you from without. This is the ultimate form of dis-empowerment. As long as you believe in this perception of life, there is no way for you to take back your creative power.'

'I know you see this, so now make the logical conclusion. The *only* way to change the equation is that you start acknowledging that in every situation you face in life, you *do* have a choice, you do have more than one option. It may be perfectly true that you have no physical power to change the outer situation. In your case, I am not saying that by changing your mind, you will magically bring your leg back.'

'Regardless of what the outer situation is like, there is more than one possible way to react to that situation. By acknowledging that you have more than one option for how you react to the situation – how you look at the situation – you start taking back your power. You start digging yourself out of the black hole of powerlessness.'

'My Son, look at yourself. When we met in the marketplace, you told me that your anger was directed at all these outer conditions. You thought that your outer situation – and the way you experienced your outer situation – was determined by the enemy, luck, fate, the Machine, life or God.'

'What you are telling me now is that you have recognized that your outer situation was not exclusively caused by these outer conditions. It was – at least to some degree – also caused by choices *you* made.'

'Do you see that this is a momentous shift away from you being powerless? Do you see that this means you have already started to take back the power to change your life experience through your own choices?'

The Warrior answers: 'Yes, I do actually see that, but that doesn't make me feel less guilty. In fact, it makes me feel *more* guilty because when I was projecting that my situation was caused by outside factors, I felt little guilt, I just felt anger. Now that I recognize that my own choices were partly to blame for my situation, I obviously have to blame myself.'

'Why,' the Master says, 'does taking responsibility for your choices mean you have to blame yourself?'

The Warrior is taken aback and stammers: 'I…well, I mean, I hate that my leg is amputated and if it is the result of a choice I made, then I obviously made a very stupid choice…

how could I not feel guilty about that? In my upbringing it was instilled in me that I should feel guilty for making mistakes.'

The Master says: 'What if I told you that both the choice to go to war and your reaction to it are controlled by the Machine?'

'Step back and think about this. You have started to see that you grew up in an environment in which most people are controlled by the Machine. You have started to see that the Machine controls people by pulling them into struggling, including struggling to control other people. The Machine has made people believe that the only way to control their inner situation is to control other people. Everyone is constantly seeking to control others. Is not war the ultimate way for human beings to seek to control each other? In war, you seek to get the enemy to submit. You are willing to destroy those who will not submit—or destroy yourself rather than give up your quest for control.'

'You grew up in an environment in which society and people around you were always seeking to control you. Not necessarily in a malicious or deliberate way, but they were trying to control you as a way to maintain the sense of being in control of their life experience.'

'You did not understand what was going on, but you experienced that some external force was seeking to control you. You resented it but felt powerless to stop it. The result was that you built a personal spiral of anger energy that eventually started controlling your conscious mind. It was because of this anger spiral that you made the choice to go to war. You were looking at life through the perception filter of anger. It seemed perfectly logical to you that if you destroyed the enemy, you would bring back peace.'

'What I want you to see here is that it *was* indeed perfectly logical what you saw. Yet it was logical *only* because you viewed the situation through that particular perception filter.'

'You made the choice to go to war, and you then had to face the consequence of losing your leg. Again, you "see" that this consequence can never be undone, but this seems logical *only* because you are also looking at it through the same perception filter. But let that rest for now.'

'You have now started separating yourself from your perception filter, but your mind is still partly colored by the filter. This means that as you begin to acknowledge that losing your leg was a result of a choice you made, you are looking at this admission through your old perception filter. Through that filter, it does seem perfectly logical that you made a wrong choice. It seems equally logical that you should feel guilty for making this choice.'

'In reality, this is only so because you are looking at the situation through the same perception filter that caused you to make the choice that created the situation. The *only* way out of the human struggle, and the only way to self-mastery, is to free your mind from *any* of the perception filters that make up the Machine. You do remember, do you not, that you said you want to be free from the Machine?'

'Yes, Master,' the Warrior says, 'and I still want to be free more than anything else.'

'Good, then I need you to recognize that the path to self-mastery means that you move from being powerless to taking back full power over your mind. This means you must go through several phases, as no one can complete the journey in one leap. The first stage is that you start taking responsibility for your situation as – at least partially – the result of choices you made.'

'It is inevitable that as you do this, you will feel a sense of guilt over having made what you will see as wrong or bad choices. No one who has ever walked the path of self-mastery

4 | Seeing the "Enemy" Within

has avoided this phase. Yet what have I taught you about energy?'

'In the collective consciousness are many of these spirals or vortexes of fear-based energy. Anger is one and guilt is another. The Machine often controls people by overwhelming their individual minds by a collective spiral of anger energy. The anger blinds you to the extent that you take aggressive action aimed at controlling other people or destroying those who will not be controlled.'

'The Machine gets you to respond from anger, but it has also set up a scale for evaluating the outcome of the choices made in anger. If you fail to control others, the standard says you have failed. If you experience that in your quest to destroy others you end up destroying yourself, the Machine says *you* have failed.'

'As you face the consequences of the choices you make in anger, the Machine seeks to overwhelm you with a sense of guilt and blame. The Machine can then control you by trying to make you run away from or compensate for the feeling of guilt. This also prevents you from questioning your perception.'

'In order to start breaking free of the spiral of making choices through anger, you have to take responsibility for your choices. This means you will inevitably become the target for the guilt and blame spirals. By becoming conscious of this and by using the tools for transforming fear-based energy, you can free yourself from the downward pull of guilt and blame.'

'You cannot escape it completely, but by being aware of it as a phase, you can move through it much more quickly. In your case, you have the advantage of being in a community where the other students have already moved through this phase. They will be very happy to help you transform your own energy.'

'This will be your next assignment. Then we will talk more about how you take command over your life experience and begin to change the consequences that the Machine will have you believe cannot be undone.'

5 | THE SUBTLE WORKINGS OF THE HUMAN MIND

Time passes and the Warrior practices the techniques for consuming the energy spiral of guilt. One day, as the students are sitting in the assembly hall, the Master says to the Warrior:

'My Son, I see that you have now consumed most of your personal guilt spiral so we can take the next step. Do you remember that some time ago I asked you: "What are you?" Do you remember your answer?'

'Yes, it was that I am not the body but a non-material mind.'

'Good,' the Master continues, 'and what exactly does this mean? It means that none of us are what we were brought up to see ourselves as being. We live in a world that is not the way we were brought up to seeing it.'

'One of the most subtle effects of the Machine is that it makes us believe that the material world has some kind of objective or independent reality. Because matter seems so solid to our physical senses, we think it is independent of the mind.'

'Almost a century ago, some physicists developed a new branch of science, called quantum mechanics. They came up with the first scientific challenge to the view that the matter world has an existence that is independent of the mind. They discovered that at the most fundamental level of matter, what we see is not something that exists independently of our minds. What we see is *co-created* by our minds.'

'What quantum physics has proven is what a few spiritual teachers have been saying for thousands of years. What I have taken you towards is the most fundamental realization one can come to as a human being. This is the one realization that can set you free from the clutches of the Machine, from the collective beast that rules the material world with an iron fist.'

'What is this realization? It is that – contrary to what our senses, our outer minds and the collective mind are telling us – matter is not *cause* but only *effect*. The relationship between matter and mind is that matter is not the cause of what happens in the mind. The mind is the cause of what happens in matter. The deeper reason being that the matter world is actually created by mind.'

'Freeing your mind from the persuasive and aggressive illusion that matter is cause is the main task for any student who wants to be free from the Machine. It is not an easy task because there is a giant energy spiral that seeks to force your mind to stay focused on the seeming reality of matter. It is very strong and very aggressive in seeking to prevent your mind from escaping its magnetic pull.'

'The deeper reality is that everything you see in the matter world was created by some kind of mind. As a human being on earth you are meant to use your creative powers to consciously co-create your situation. What has happened to most people is that due to the persuasive and aggressive illusion created by the Machine, people have forgotten or denied their creative powers. Instead of *consciously* co-creating their situation, most people are *unconsciously* co-creating their situation.'

'It is precisely because of this that most people believe that the material conditions they encounter are the cause of their state of mind. When you look beyond surface appearances, you see that human beings have collectively co-created the current struggle on this planet. They have done this through the power of their minds.'

'Because they have forgotten how the mind works, they now think the material conditions they have created have some independent existence, meaning the very people who created them do not have the power to change them. They think they can only react to these conditions, and thus the *outer* conditions determine their *inner* conditions.'

'The absolutely *only* way to escape the clutches of the Machine is to use the higher faculties of your mind to continually question this illusion until you once again awaken to the fact that you are not a *mechanical* being but a *creative* being. Nothing in the material world can force you to react a certain way. Freedom from the Machine means that you are free to choose any reaction you want to any circumstance you encounter in the material world. Nothing in matter forces what happens in your mind.'

'By practicing the techniques for invoking love-based energy, you can create a shield of protection around your mind. You can also begin to consume the energy spirals inside your mind that are forming the dead weight that gives the collective beast something in you upon which it can exert its pull. You have already been doing this and you will become more focused on doing so.'

'This will take you towards the point where you begin to realize that your mind is not reacting to independent conditions in the matter world. The conditions in the matter world were created by mind and your mind is reacting to conditions in the mind. It may seem as if your mind cannot change conditions in matter, but surely your mind can change conditions in mind.'

Matter does not actually exist

The Warrior looks perplexed and the Master asks him to formulate his question. The Warrior says: 'I don't understand how we human beings create our situation. I mean, I have read that some people speculate that the entire material universe is not real but is created by the mind, is that what you are saying?'

The Master replies: 'You have heard of Albert Einstein and his theory of relativity. Do you know what this theory actually says?'

The Warrior answers: 'I think it says that matter can be converted into energy. So you can split the Uranium atom and release the energy in a reactor or an atomic bomb?'

'That is the common view,' the Master says, 'but it is only a partial understanding of what Einstein's formula actually says. The famous formula, $E=mc^2$, actually says that matter does not exist. Matter or mass is a form of energy that has taken on a greater density than what we normally see as flowing or vibrating energy. A rock appears more dense or solid than a sunbeam. Most people will say that a rock is matter and a sunbeam is energy, and they would say matter and energy are two fundamentally different things or elements.'

'What Einstein discovered is that matter and energy are not fundamentally different. What we call matter is simply energy that has crossed a threshold so that it appears more solid than flowing energy. This appearance of solidity is only seen by the human senses. Do you remember being on an airfield and seeing them start up an engine with propellers? As the propeller is turning slowly, your eyes can see the individual propeller blades so you can see that there is space between them. As the propeller spins more quickly, your eyes can no longer pick out the individual blades. The propeller now appears as a solid disc with no space. This is a crude illustration of how matter fools our physical senses into seeing it as solid.'

'A rock is still created from energy. We might even say that a rock is the energy of a beam of light that has been condensed or lowered in vibration so that our senses can no longer see its vibrations but detect it as a solid and unchanging substance.'

'I know this seems confusing at first, but I ask you to compare it to what you have experienced as you have been invoking love-based energy. You have directly experienced that it is possible for you to invoke a stream of high-frequency energy that can consume or transform the low-frequency, fear-based energy in your mind. How is it even possible for you to do this? '

How light becomes matter

'Einstein's formula contains the answer. Do you know what c^2 stands for?'

'I think c is the speed of light and Einstein used it as a constant to make his equation work,' the Warrior replies.

The Master continues: 'Yes, and as you know, the speed of light is a very high number. Einstein's formula truly says that the material universe was created by a form of energy that vibrates at such a high level that it is beyond what we call material energy. This energy was then reduced in vibration by a very large reduction factor. The speed of light squared is a very large number, which means the original energy was exposed to a huge reduction in order to take on the appearance of solid matter. Is it any wonder our crude physical senses cannot detect this primordial energy?'

'The matter universe was created by and is upheld by a "stream" of energy that is being reduced in vibration. After the energy has been reduced to the level of vibration that makes up the material spectrum, the energy is then given the forms that we detect as solid matter. How does this happen?'

'Before Einstein, there were two prevailing theories. One was that an almighty God in some remote heaven had instantly created the material universe in its present form. The other was that a purely mechanical evolutionary process, essentially a game of chance, had created the current universe with no conscious design. While both of these theories are still being given life-support by their faithful adherents, quantum physics has invalidated both of them.'

'Quantum physics has proven that all material forms are made from very small entities, normally called subatomic particles. These so-called particles are very confusing entities in that they can behave as both solid particles and vibrating waves.'

'The revolutionary discovery of quantum physics is that the appearance of subatomic particles is a process that must involve some kind of mind. Before Einstein, scientists believed they could observe a subatomic particle and their minds would not influence the particle. They took pride in this and thought it was what made science objective, as opposed to religion.'

'Quantum physicists discovered that when they observed a subatomic particle, they were not simply observing something that existed independently of their minds. Their minds became an intricate part of the process, meaning they were actively co-creating the particle they observed. The particle did not exist as a material entity until they made the observation.'

5 | *The Subtle Workings of the Human Mind*

'When you compare this to Einstein, you see that the material world is created from a "stream" of energy that is gradually lowered in vibration. As this energy crosses a certain threshold, it "enters" the spectrum of the vibrations that make up the material realm. We can say that the pure energy becomes a subatomic particle that can be used to build all of the matter forms we see with our senses.'

'Quantum physicists say that before the energy appears as a material particle, it exists in a realm of probability. In this state, it is not yet material, meaning it is not locked into a particular form. It has the potential to take on different forms.'

'As the energy crosses the threshold, it takes on a particular form and appears as a specific particle. It is this process that *must* involve some kind of mind. Physicists have proven beyond any doubt that the human mind can be part of this process. How does this work?'

How minds create matter

'This could be described in different ways, but here is a straightforward explanation. Our minds have the ability to be conduits for energy from a higher level of vibration. As this energy streams through our minds, we affect the energy. Before it enters our minds, the energy exists in a state of probability where it can take on different forms. As the energy flows through our minds, the probabilities are reduced to just one, and the energy takes on a specific form.'

'The revolutionary fact discovered by quantum physicists is that it is the state of your mind that determines which form the energy takes on. Your mind is selecting which one of the potentially large number of probabilities becomes manifest as a material form. If you are blinded by a personal spiral, you might be unable to see the many potential outcomes. You think you have only one choice.'

'What do I mean when I say most people have forgotten that they are creative beings? I mean that people have forgotten their ability to bring energy of a higher vibration into the material spectrum. When you bring such energy, many of the seemingly unchangeable physical conditions can indeed be changed, at least over time. You have proven this by invoking light to heal your wounds from the past. When you forget this ability, you are confined to seeking to change your life by using only the energy that has already been lowered to the material spectrum. This will severely limit your creative powers.'

'The Machine is made from energies that vibrate in the material spectrum. It is even made from the lower levels of such energies, namely fear-based energies. The Machine can survive by getting people to do two things. One is to keep them ignorant of their potential to bring creative energies into the physical spectrum. The other is by getting them to unconsciously take creative energies and lower them to the fear-based spectrum. It does this by keeping them trapped in the never-ending struggle against each other. The Machine can survive only by upholding the collective illusion that created and sustains the Machine. If a critical mass of individuals freed their minds from this illusion, it would gradually bring about the end of the Machine.'

Did human beings create the universe?

'Let me return to your question of whether human beings created the universe. Let us look at the two prevailing theories. According to some religions, a perfect God created the entire universe and this happened instantly. According to the religion of materialism, there is no mind beyond the material. The universe was created through an unconscious process that gradually – and with no goal or design – led to the complexity we see today.'

'The higher understanding that quantum physics and ancient mysticism demands from us is that these theories do not give the full picture. Clearly, science has proven that the material universe did not appear instantly in its present form. There is a gradual process leading from simple to more complex forms. What is the purpose of this process? It is to give us an opportunity to grow in self-awareness by being part of the creative process.'

'As quantum physics has proven, matter is made from energy that takes on concrete forms and this process *must* involve some kind of mind. Clearly, the process of the formation of matter started before human beings existed and thus we have not created the universe with our minds. There is a large number of self-aware beings who exist in a higher vibrational spectrum. They are the beings who have created the material universe in its basic form.'

'We human beings are also self-aware minds, but we have entered a material body and focused our self-awareness around this body and the material universe. We have chosen to do this in order to grow in self-awareness. We grow by becoming increasingly aware of our co-creative abilities. Our minds are designed to be conduits for high-frequency energy. As we lower it in vibration, we give the energy concrete, material forms.'

'As we experience the material conditions we have co-created, we can use it to assess whether they are the highest form of expression we are capable of or whether we could create something higher. How do we co-create something higher? By acknowledging that our present creation is an expression of our minds and then engaging in the process you have been following, namely consciously purifying our minds and expanding our sense of self.'

'Human beings have been part of the co-creative process of earth for much longer than acknowledged by both science and religion. We have used our co-creative abilities to create the current conditions of lack, limitations and struggle. Because we have forgotten the true creative powers of our minds, we have forgotten that we have created current conditions and that what we have created, we can also uncreate. We have come to believe that we are the helpless victims of what we have actually co-created. We think that our own creation was imposed upon us by an angry God in the sky or an unconscious process of evolution.'

'This is what has created the Machine. It is people's unwillingness to question the basic illusion of matter as cause that upholds the Machine. If you want to be free from the Machine, you need to question this illusion, which is precisely what you have been practicing.'

The slavery of the subconscious mind

The Warrior says: 'I do experience that my mind is capable of receiving this flow of energy, and I can direct it. I can see how I used to direct all of my creative energy into this spiral of anger. You and the other students have now taught me I have a choice and that I can create an upward spiral instead of a downward one. Yet I still don't fully see how my mind creates by using energy. Can you help me understand this better?'

The Master replies: 'When you first came here, your attention was directed outwards, thinking external conditions were the cause of your misery. Since then, you have begun clearing the low-frequency energy from your mind. As a result, you have started to see things, such as your feelings of guilt, that were previously hidden beneath the threshold of conscious awareness. We can also say that you have been moving the threshold of conscious awareness so that you are now conscious of things that used to be subconscious.'

'Most human beings have a very high threshold of conscious awareness, which means they do not see very deeply into their own minds. Most of their minds are in the subconscious realm and that is why it is so easy for the Machine to control them. People do not see how they are being controlled because the mechanisms of control hide in the subconscious.'

'Imagine that you are in a boat on the sea. Suddenly an edible fish pops up from beneath the surface and you catch it. Then an ugly, slimy monster pops up and you seek to avoid it. For most people, their minds are beneath the surface and they have no idea why certain thoughts and feelings suddenly pop up. Such people can only react to what their own subconscious minds throw at them, but they have no control over what their minds produce internally and how their minds are affected by external circumstances.'

'You may say that such people are still making choices at the conscious level, but the problem is that they can only choose between the impulses that rise out of the depth of the subconscious mind. If all of these impulses are affected by the Machine, how will you have true freedom of choice? The obvious conclusion is that in order to free yourself from the Machine and become empowered to make truly free choices, you must lower the threshold of conscious awareness and begin to look into the subconscious layers of the mind.'

'Scientists have asked the question of whether the world is still there when no one is looking. The answer is that there is always someone who is looking. At the personal level, your subconscious mind is always looking. You may be thinking that if you are asleep or unconscious, then you are not looking and thus you are not co-creating your misery. The reality is that your mind has subconscious layers and they are always co-creating your life experience.'

'Many people have attempted to escape their negative life experience by dulling the conscious mind with chemicals. When they return to some form of conscious awareness, their situation has not improved but often grown worse. The reason is that while your conscious mind was unconscious, your subconscious mind was still co-creating your life circumstances. As soon as your conscious mind returns to consciousness, you are faced with what your subconscious mind has co-created while you had checked out.'

'Many people in the world are trying to prove that by dulling their minds, their problems will one day go away. It never works because even if you go out of the physical body – temporarily or permanently – you can never escape your subconscious mind. There is only one escape. It is to start looking into the subconscious part of your mind and take conscious control over what is going on there.'

The four levels of the human mind

The Master continues: 'Let me explain the creative process of the mind by beginning at the physical level. This is looking at the flow backwards, but it is the easiest way to relate it to your personal experience.'

'In your own case, you experienced that the enemy attacked your nation and that your leader called for those who would go fight the enemy. Based on this, you made the conscious decision

5 | The Subtle Workings of the Human Mind

to join the army and go to war. This decision led to the very harsh consequence that you lost one leg. In your mind, there is nothing that can be done to change this fact and thus there is seemingly nothing that can be done to change the impact that the physical consequence has on your life experience.'

'If you allow your attention to continue to be focused on the physical level, then there really *is* nothing you can do to change your situation. What have you been doing since you came here? You have pushed back the level of conscious awareness and started to see that the decision made at the conscious level did not just pop up randomly from the depths of the subconscious. There is a process, there are patterns, in the subconscious mind. When you make those processes conscious, you can change them and change your life experience.'

'In your case, you have discovered that there is a spiral of anger that has been built since childhood. It was the accumulation of emotional energy that pulled your conscious mind into going to war. The decisions you make at the physical level are very deeply affected by what happens at a higher level of the mind, namely that of feelings. The options you see at the conscious level will be limited by the spirals that exist in the emotional part of the mind. In your case, your anger spiral prevented you from seeing a non-violent way to respond to your nation being attacked. Your leader and many of your countrymen had their vision limited in a similar way, which explains why your nation went to war.'

'We now see that physical actions spring from feelings, but where do feelings come from? Do you remember what you were thinking after the enemy had attacked your nation?'

The Warrior replies: 'I was thinking that the attack was unjustifiable and that it was necessary for us to respond decisively in order to prevent more attacks. I thought these people did not have the same humanitarian values we do and thus they would never respect any form of negotiation. They hate us and the only way to stop more attacks was to make them fear the consequences.'

The Master says: 'Good. I will refrain from discussing your thinking on this point because I want to show you that your feelings spring from an even higher level of the mind, namely that of thoughts. Do you recognize that it was your thinking that made you decide that it was justifiable for your nation to go to war? Do you see that on one hand your humanitarian values say that killing is wrong, but on the other hand you reasoned that because of what the enemy had done, it was necessary and justifiable for you to destroy the enemy in order to preserve your nation?'

'Yes,' the Warrior replies, 'I did think that although my religion says "Thou shalt not kill," in this case it was both necessary and justifiable to kill the enemy.'

'Good,' the Master says, 'then you recognize that it was your thinking that justified that you expressed your personal anger – an anger spiral that the enemy had not created – by taking it out on the enemy?'

'Yes, I do see that, but…'

The Master interrupts: 'No, no, I do not want to debate your reasoning. I simply want to show you that at the physical level, you made a decision. This decision was triggered by your feelings of anger, and the feelings were very much tied to certain thoughts. Do you see the sequence of actions springing from feelings that spring from thoughts?'

'Yes Master, I do see this now.'

'Then you also begin to see that for you to control what is happening at the conscious level of your mind, you must begin to look into the subconscious, you must begin to make the subconscious conscious. What you have been doing is to invoke love-based energy to consume much of the fear-based energy that formed your personal spirals of anger and guilt. One effect of such maelstroms of energy is that they prevent you from seeing the thoughts behind them.'

'If you cannot see the thoughts, you cannot change them. If you cannot change the thoughts, how will you ever overcome the emotional spirals? You can invoke love-based energy to consume the emotional energy, but if you do not change your thinking, you will produce new emotional energy as fast, or almost as fast, as you can transform it.'

Your sense of who you are

'In the coming time, we will use the new clarity in your mind to examine your thinking. I first want to make you aware that above the level of thoughts there is another level of the mind. I would like you to think back at the situation where you had been wounded and you were lying in the sand waiting to die. You told me that it was as if you went outside your body and outer mind. You saw everything with a new clarity.'

'Now tune in to how you experienced that situation. Do you recognize that what actually happened was that there was a part of your mind that stepped outside of not only your feelings and thoughts, but even something deeper?'

The Warrior replies: 'Yes, I see what you are saying. It was almost like I stepped outside of my normal personality and I was seeing it all as unreal. But I don't know exactly what that means?'

The Master says: 'Think about what you had done as you joined the army, received training and went to war. As you said yourself, you turned yourself into the "perfect killing machine." Can you see that during this process you built on to the sense of identity you had built as you grew up? Can you see that you built a sense of identity as a warrior who was justified in killing others even though doing so is against your religion? Can you see that this sense of identity of being a warrior could override humanitarian concerns?'

'Yes,' the Warrior replies thoughtfully, 'I see this very clearly now. When I was in my warrior identity, killing was perfectly justified and I never needed to reflect on it. When I was wounded, I went out of my warrior identity and I now saw how I had been fooled by the Machine into going to war and killing others.'

How energy flows in the mind

The Master continues: 'My Son, the insight you now have is that there are four levels of the human mind. The highest level is the level of your identity, your sense of self in relation to the material world. This level defines the parameters for how you see yourself, and thereby it also sets limitations for the next level down, namely that of your thinking. While you looked at yourself and life through the filter of your warrior identity, there were certain thoughts you would never have. There were certain ideas it was not necessary to think about, certain things you did not need to question.'

'Your warrior self defined limits for your thinking. This prevented you from asking the questions of whether what you did through the warrior self was what you wanted to do in the long term. In your case, your warrior self made you think you were invincible, and this prevented you from considering when it was time to leave. It even made you so careless that you became wounded by a bomb that a more careful soldier could have avoided.'

'The thinking produced by your warrior self set certain parameters for your feelings. You often felt anger against the enemy. This helped you carry out your actions, even helping you survive in combat. Yet this also kept you trapped in feeling it was necessary to stay in the war. The feelings of your warrior self also prevented you from reacting differently to being wounded and what happened after you returned.'

'What you experienced as you were lying in the sand was that you went outside your warrior self, but this self was not instantly dissolved. It was still there, and that is why – as you returned home – you were in a schizophrenic state of still carrying your warrior self with you while knowing it was not really who you are. You reacted to being in civilian life in a way that prevented you from finding any kind of peace. After all, how can a warrior be at peace when he is not in battle? Do you see this?'

'Yes, Master,' the Warrior replies, 'you have once again opened my eyes. I totally see how I was trapped in this warrior self and I see I am not actually this self. But this leaves me to ponder who or what I actually am?'

The Master says: 'That is a question I will help you answer, but it will take time. We still need to remove the remnants of the warrior self and the self you built before joining the army.'

The self that is beyond time and space

'For now, I want you to consider what you actually experienced in the desert. You said you experienced yourself as a mind that was beyond time and space. Throughout the ages, many people have had such mystical experiences. They are the foundation for the path that I and other spiritual teachers teach.'

'The reason you can have such experiences is that your sense of identity is not who you are. I have said that there are four levels of the mind, and together they form the vehicle through which you are expressing yourself in the material world.'

'There is a stream of energy that is flowing through your mind from a higher realm. As this undifferentiated energy flows through the four levels of the mind, it gradually takes on form based on what is found – the thoughts and energy spirals – at those four levels. This is how you co-create by superimposing mental images upon the undifferentiated energy. The energy can do nothing but take on the forms that exist at the four levels of your mind.'

'This we will explore later, but for now I want to return to the fact that the four levels of the mind form a vehicle through which you express yourself in this world. You are *not* the vehicle, you are simply using it. You get into this soul vehicle as you get into a car. You never think you *become* the car by getting into it, but because most people have forgotten who they are, they think they have become the soul vehicle.'

'What are you really? You are what you experienced, namely a mind that is not limited by time and space. I often call this the Conscious You, but this is simply a name that indicates it is the part of you that can be conscious of its own existence. It is what makes you conscious and gives you a sense that you are an individual being.'

How the creative flow was shut down

The Master continues: 'In the ideal scenario, the Conscious You is aware that it is a creative being, a co-creator. It receives a stream of high-frequency energy from a higher source, which some call your spiritual self or higher self. I call it your I AM Presence.'

'As the energy streams into the four levels of your outer mind, it is gradually reduced in vibration and it starts to take on the form of a mental image. This begins in your identity body, becomes more concrete in your mental body, receives momentum in your emotional body and then takes on its most concrete form at the level of the physical mind and body.'

'In the ideal scenario, you know that you are not actually here on earth in order to produce particular physical results. You are here to have certain experiences that expand your consciousness, expand your sense of self, expand your sense of what you can do with your co-creative powers. Nothing that happens at the physical level matters. What matters is what happens at the higher levels of the mind and how that affects your sense of self.'

'Sometime in the past, you became a victim of the deception that created the Machine. You came to believe that instead of being a co-creator who is connected to a higher source, you are a separate being that exists independently. This caused you to forget your co-creative powers. Instead, you started seeing yourself as a reactive being who can only influence your situation through the powers of the physical body and physical mind. Some people even came to believe that they are the products of the material world instead of being co-creators. This is the ultimate denial of your creative potential.'

'When we look at your situation as it is today, we see that from an overall perspective, you still have your co-creative potential. Your I AM Presence exists in a realm of vibrations that is beyond the four levels of the material universe. Nothing that has ever happened on earth has destroyed or limited your I AM Presence. The only thing that has happened is that the Conscious You has forgotten its true identity of being connected to the I AM Presence. Instead, the Conscious You has started identifying itself with and as the sense of self that is a product of the physical, emotional, mental and identity levels of the mind.'

'In reality, the Conscious You is who it is. In its own inner experience, it is who it *thinks* it is. If you think you are a separate being who has limited creative powers, then that is how you behave. In that case, your experience in the matter world will validate and reinforce your sense of self.'

'The collective mind, that was formed by humankind after people became blinded by the illusion of separation, has become very strong. It is difficult for individual minds to escape its gravitational pull. The only way to free yourself from the Machine is to free your mind from the gravitational pull while at the same time shifting your sense of identity. You cannot *pull* yourself free through the use of force. You must remove the elements, the beliefs and energy spirals, in your subconscious mind that the Machine can pull upon.'

'In reality, you are still a co-creator, but currently your creative potential is being blocked. It is being blocked by spirals in the four levels of the lower mind. These spirals are partly made up of low-frequency energy and partly by illusions, limiting beliefs. It is these internal spirals that tie you to the collective spiral and give the Machine power over you. The Machine uses them to pull you into reactionary patterns that reinforce your internal spirals. The Machine wants to make sure you can never break free from these patterns and reclaim your identity as a creative being who has the potential to create your own life experience.'

'We have taught you techniques for invoking the high-frequency energy that can lessen the gravitational pull on your conscious mind. As you do this, you can begin to look for the beliefs that are the causes behind the energy spirals at the four levels of the mind. Once you see a belief and see that it is an illusion, you can replace it with a higher realization, and then that particular spiral is dissolved.'

'This will allow you to make use of a greater portion of your co-creative powers. You can use them to improve your situation and to work on the next limiting spiral. This can turn your life into an upward path. By your work over these months, you have already built a powerful momentum. We now need to direct this into taking a look at the spirals at the higher levels of the mind.'

'We will begin with your emotional mind. You have been working on invoking love-based energy to reduce the energy spirals caused by guilt and anger. I want you to focus on these two spirals. After each session of invoking love-based energy, I want you to go into the vortex of emotional energy and ask yourself what is the belief that started the spiral of guilt and anger. You go into the feeling and then you consider what you actually believe that causes you to feel guilt and anger. We will then talk again when you have attained greater clarity on this.'

6 | FREEDOM FROM ANGER AND GUILT

Time passes. One day, the Master asks the Warrior to describe his insights. The Warrior answers: 'It took me a long time to consume the energy that clouded my vision. It was only because I had already experienced that invoking energy actually works that I kept doing it long enough to feel any improvement.'

'The first belief I uncovered was a kind of two-headed belief that on the one hand I am powerless and on the other hand this makes me worthless or inferior. Underneath that was this feeling of hopelessness, a sense that I simply can't change my physical circumstances through the powers of my mind and that what you are trying to teach me is nonsense, that it simply can't be true.'

'Very good,' the Master says, 'these are beliefs that all of us have to deal with.'

'But how do I deal with the feeling? Can I reason with it?' asks the Warrior.

The Master replies: 'You cannot ever reason with a feeling. A feeling is a feeling, an emotion is energy in motion. Once an energy impulse has entered the emotional body, it is beyond reason.'

'Many people in the modern world have become so accustomed to using the analytical, intellectual mind that they think this is the only way to deal with feelings. They reason that they should not have certain feelings, and then they seek to overcome the feelings by analyzing them. This is doomed to failure. In fact, analyzing your feelings only increases your sense of hopelessness and frustration.'

'Once an energy impulse has entered the frequency spectrum of the emotional body, the energy will continue to move in its predefined direction until it is either exhausted, redirected or until you transform it into a higher form of energy. An emotion is energy in motion. You can use this by invoking higher energies that cause the emotion to be accelerated to a higher level of vibration. Fear-based energy can be accelerated into love-based energy, as you have already experienced.'

'Once you have accelerated enough emotional energy that it is no longer blinding, you can begin to look for the belief that generated the energy spiral. This belief likely will not be found in the emotional body but in the higher bodies.'

'There *are* beliefs at the emotional level, as there are beliefs at the physical level. For example, there is a belief at the physical level that the survival of your physical body is more important than the survival of the physical bodies of other people. If you find yourself in a situation where someone is threatening to kill you, as you have experienced first-hand, this belief will kick in and you will kill the other person. You will often feel justified in doing this by saying: "It was him or me." I assume you have experienced this?'

'Master, that is exactly how I justified killing people when I was at war. This allowed me to kill people without reflecting on it, and this allowed me to continue surviving—and killing.'

The Master continues: 'Yes, and war is simply an extreme example of how the Machine puts people in situations where they do things without reflecting on them. Both sides feel forced into killing the other side, but who is forcing them? If each side says the other side is forcing them to kill, what if both sides decided to no longer play the game? Of course, they can't because the Machine has caused communication between them to break down, but that is another issue.'

'As there are beliefs at the physical level, there are also some beliefs that exist at the emotional level. They do not give rise to feelings, but they reinforce feelings and give them a particular direction, giving rise to actions. These beliefs relate to what feelings you have and how you express them. In your case, taking your anger out on the enemy and feeling this was justified is one example of a belief at the emotional level.'

'Another example is your sense of feeling powerless and inferior. As emotional energy continues to accumulate, your emotional body becomes a very unpleasant place to be. At the same time the increasing intensity of the energy draws your conscious attention to it. This becomes an unsustainable situation where pressure builds until something must relieve it. You are actually fighting something inside your own emotional body, but since you cannot see that, you must find another way to deal with the emotional energy.'

'There are two common ways out. One is that there is nothing outside yourself that can become an outlet for your feelings. You reason that your situation is hopeless and you simply submit and stop fighting the tension. You become the perfect victim who believes there is no way out of your frustration. Once you have accepted that you cannot change the situation, it becomes easier to live with. Of course, you also turn yourself into a slave of your subconscious emotions and through them of the Machine.'

'The other common reaction is that you find an outlet towards which you can direct your feelings. You find a scapegoat who is supposedly the cause of your situation. Your sense of powerlessness and inferiority becomes transformed into anger. You then take your anger out on the scapegoat by taking some form of action.'

'In your case, your personal anger became directed at the enemy and you attempted to kill the enemy in order to kill the chaos in your own emotional body. What I want you to do here is to consider what kind of beliefs at the emotional level caused you to respond with anger.'

'I am not sure I understand. Can you help me get started?' the Warrior asks.

'You remember that before you went to war, you had already started to build an anger spiral?' the Master asks.

'Yes, I do remember that.'

'The enemy was not the cause of the anger because the anger was in *you*. You felt angry because of the underlying sense of being powerless and inferior. In your case, you refused to submit to this and become a victim. Instead, you turned your sense of being powerless into anger, and the anger gave you a certain sense of empowerment. This is more constructive than making yourself a passive victim. A victim cannot be helped because he or she it not willing to move. An angry person is at least moving and can thus be given a more constructive direction.'

'You can see that it was the sense of being powerless that led to the anger and that your anger gave you a sense of having power by destroying the enemy?'

'Yes, I do see that now,' the Warrior replies.

'Then what is the belief that made you react with anger instead of as a passive victim?'

'I guess I could not see any other way to react. It seemed to me that the anger was justified because of what the enemy had done.'

'Yet,' says the Master, 'we have seen that your enemies did not cause the anger, they just became the outlet for it. So what was the belief about the anger?'

'Oh, I see this, I must have believed that the anger was justified because it was the only way I could react.'

'Good,' the Master replies, 'now you are getting closer. We all have a belief in our emotional bodies that in certain situations, the only way for us to react is by feeling anger. Once we are in a situation where we feel anger, we not only feel the anger is justified, we also feel it is justified to project the anger out through actions against other people. After all, we can see no other way to respond to those kinds of situations.'

'Do you see that this pattern is the reason you went to war, and thus the indirect reason why you are sitting here with only one leg?'

The Warrior sighs: 'You are right, it was simply a stupid emotional pattern that caused me to go to war and get turned into a cripple. So how do I break free from this pattern?'

'Well,' the Master replies, 'eventually I hope to help you no longer see yourself as a cripple, but let us start with something easier. The dynamic of the situation is simple. You feel powerless and you can see no way to avoid this feeling. This causes frustration to build until you react with anger. The anger builds until you take action, and the action has certain inescapable physical consequences.'

'The key to breaking the emotional pattern is to realize that it all starts with the sense of being powerless and inferior. While these are feelings, the feelings come from beliefs that exist at the mental level of the mind, or the mental body. For example, the belief in your emotional body says your anger is justified, but the specific reasoning that seemingly justifies the anger takes place in the mental body. The next step is to have you start looking into your mental body. If I ask you to look at the thoughts behind the feelings of being powerless and inferior, what do you see?'

The Warrior thinks for some time while a frustrated expression appears on his face. He then says: 'I can't see anything. My thoughts seem to be very unclear or confused on this issue.'

'This is natural,' the Master says. 'The reason is that you have a spiral of energy in your mental body, and it is having the effect of clouding your thoughts. Again, you will use special exercises for purifying your mental body by invoking love-based energy. My students will help you do this, and when you have cleared enough energy, we will talk again. After each session where you invoke energy, I want you to observe your mind and look for the beliefs related to being powerless and inferior.'

'You need to be aware that as the emotional level of the mind has layers, so does the mental level. Most people are aware of only very superficial thoughts that relate to their material circumstances and daily lives. I am asking you to become aware of such thoughts and then start looking beyond them to the higher levels of thoughts, the ones that relate to your more subtle beliefs about life, especially about being powerless and what you can and cannot do in this world.'

Why people cannot see their thoughts

'In order to do this, you need to be aware of one of the most common patterns that prevents people from examining their thoughts without becoming involved with them. Most of the thoughts that come to your conscious mind have passed through the emotional body and are thus already tied to a feeling. This means you are instantly tempted to go into the feeling or react to it. This you need to avoid.'

'It might help you to think about these computer games where you are walking through an underground maze. Once in a while a monster jumps out at you and you have to shoot it before it kills you. A thought that reaches your conscious mind is like a monster that jumps at you from the hidden parts of the mind. Your task is *not* to shoot it but to avoid reacting to it. You do not get points for reacting to the thought; you only get points for *not* reacting.'

'As you practice this, you might find it beneficial to go back to your experience of being outside the body. This helps you to know that you are more than your thoughts and feelings. Simply ask yourself: "Am I this feeling? Am I the thought behind it?" The answer is that you are not the thought; you are not the mental aspect of your mind. It is a vehicle you are using but you are more than the vehicle.'

'What is the mental mind? You may look at it as a computer. A computer is a mechanical device that is programmed to always react the same way to the same stimuli. If you click a certain button, you get a certain reaction. The mental mind is likewise programmed to think a certain way in certain situations.'

'Beyond this, the mental mind is a computer that is programmed to think thoughts. Its function is to create thoughts and present them to the conscious mind. The function of the conscious mind is to accept or dismiss thoughts. Most people are not even aware that they have the option to dismiss thoughts. They think they have to accept all thoughts sent at them from the mental computer because they think that they are thinking them.

'I need you to come to the point where you realize that you are not thinking your thoughts. The mental mind is producing the thoughts, but you are not the mind. You are more than the mind. When you realize this, you can avoid becoming involved with the thoughts that come to you during meditation.'

'You realize that these are simply thoughts that the mental mind is sending at you and you dismiss all of them. As you become able to dismiss the superficial thoughts that come at you, you will begin to experience the higher level of thoughts. There will be many types of such thoughts, but I want you to dismiss all of them except the ones that relate to your abilities and inabilities, meaning why you feel powerless. I do not want you to engage such thoughts, but to simply notice and remember them. After you practice this for a time, we will talk again.'

7 | FREEDOM FROM VALUE JUDGMENTS

After some time, the Master again addresses the Warrior during a meeting in the assembly hall: 'My Son, I see that you have now cleared out some of the dross in the mental mind. Tell me what you discovered about feeling powerless.'

The Warrior replies: 'This was difficult, Master. There were just so many thoughts, but as you said, I eventually learned to dismiss most of them. What I discovered was that I feel powerless mainly because I am afraid of making wrong choices that lead to very harsh physical consequences, such as losing my leg.'

'Even beyond physical consequences, I fear making wrong choices that will condemn me to future suffering. There is a part of me that rejects the common idea of hell, but I am still afraid of making such a severe mistake that it can never be undone. I do not feel sure that I can tell the difference between right and wrong choices. Since I am not sure how to make only right choices and avoid wrong choices, it is as if a part of me does not want to make any choices at all.'

'There is something in me that says that if I don't make *any* choices, I cannot make any *wrong* choices, and that is safest. Of course, I realize that making no choices is not actually possible in a world that forces me to make choices. I also realize that my reluctance to make choices can only make me feel powerless.'

The Master replies: 'Excellent. You have achieved great clarity and you have put your finger on an important aspect of the human dilemma, namely that there are so many situations in this world that make us feel like we have no good choice or no choice at all. We feel paralyzed and don't know how to get ourselves out of the impasse.'

'Let me give you a simple method for removing yourself from such a catch-22. I hear you saying that the heart of the problem is that there is something called *right* choices and something called *wrong* choices, is that correct?'

'Yes, Master.'

'Good, then I ask you: What is the foundation for saying that some choices are right and some are wrong, what is behind this consideration?'

The Warrior looks perplexed, thinks for a while, then says: 'Master, I have learned that you always want me to go beyond what seems obvious to most people; you want me to question what most people do not question. Are you saying I should question why we always evaluate our choices based on a standard of right and wrong?'

'My Son, you have learned well. You used the word I was wanting you to see, namely "standard." Before you can evaluate whether a choice is right or wrong, you must have accepted three underlying premises. One is that it is possible or necessary to define a standard for evaluating choices. The second is that such a standard can have only two options, two polarities, and that they are exact opposites. The third premise is that it is necessary to evaluate choices based on this standard. Do you begin to see this?'

'Yes Master, but surely we have all been brought up to accept that our society has defined a standard for right and wrong and that we need to live our lives according to it. Are you saying this is wrong?'

The Master replies: 'My Son, not to play on words, but I am not saying anything is "wrong." I am simply trying to help you see that if you want to get yourself out of a situation where you feel powerless, you need to do two things. One is to identify the normally unseen premises or assumptions in the situation. The other is to question them. Once you have identified the premises and questioned them, you will see a way out of your paralysis.'

'You are entirely correct that we have all been brought up to accept a standard imposed by our society. Most people would say that this is perfectly necessary and beneficial. They would say a society cannot function without a standard.'

'My reply would be that it is correct that a society must have a standard, but that this standard needs to evolve over time. History is littered with examples of societies that refused to question their standard, often because they refused to question the belief system upon which the standard was based. Time has proven that all such societies will eventually be relegated to the dustbin of history. In your personal case, you grew up in a society which is based on a belief system that says killing is wrong. At the same time this society has a standard which says that in some situations killing is right. This kind of schizophrenic standard is precisely what cannot endure. If not questioned, it will inevitably lead any society into a situation where it must either change or die. Some societies change while others die. None can escape the challenge.'

'Nevertheless, let us not get lost in seeking to change the world, but let us focus on changing ourselves. In your case, you feel that having to evaluate your choices based on a standard of right and wrong is paralyzing you. How can you move out of this impasse?'

'You can begin by realizing that from childhood, you have been programmed by the Machine to accept a standard that is designed to create maximum conflict within yourself and put you in maximum conflict with other people. This increases the potential that your entire life will be swallowed up by the seeming necessity or inevitability of fighting other people. It was this standard that caused you to go to war. If it had not been for your injury, you would still be engaged in fighting others. Do you see this?'

The Warrior thinks carefully, then says: 'I see that you are right. If I had not been injured, I would have continued to fight in the war for some years, and then I would have accepted a position in the military where I would have been fighting away from the battlefield for the rest of my life. This would have made it virtually impossible for me to question some of the things that you have helped me question. I would have remained trapped in the action-reaction game of the Machine.'

The Master says: 'Perhaps there is a hidden opportunity in even some of the most seemingly tragic and painful situations we encounter in life? Perhaps, we could even begin to see such situations as a way for life to communicate to us that there is something we need to question? Perhaps they are an opportunity to step back, look at our deeper beliefs and question some of the normally unseen premises that control our lives? Perhaps doing this is the only key to greater freedom?'

The Warrior replies: 'You are right Master, but before I came here and learned how to reduce the emotional energy that caused me so much pain, I would not have been able to accept that you are right.'

'And that is why I did not ask you to consider this until I saw that you had overcome enough of the pain so you could start looking at your situation without looking through the filter that is so colored by the pain.'

Do we need a standard?

The Master continues: 'Now back to the topic of a standard. I have taught you that the purpose of life is to raise your consciousness, your sense of self. Based on this, we can create a "standard" for evaluating how far people have come in this process. This is not a black-and-white value-driven standard with only two options but a graded classification based on people's level of consciousness. What have I taught you is the goal of the process of raising your consciousness?'

'It is that I become self-sufficient by taking full responsibility for my own choices.'

'Correct, so with that in mind, let us take a look at humankind. Some people are at such a low level of self-awareness that they are unwilling to take any kind of responsibility for making their own choices. Such people want an external authority to give them a standard that says that when you do this and don't do that, you are always right and never wrong. History is full of societies in which a centralized authority attempted to define such a standard and make all their citizens follow it without ever questioning it. As you well know, some of these societies committed incredible atrocities. Only when you accept the standard of an external authority, and never question it, can you force men, women and children into a gas chamber.'

'Why have some nations transcended totalitarian forms of government and developed a democratic form of government? In a democracy, the majority of the population must be willing to take some responsibility for making their own choices. What you have seen in many democratic nations is a breakdown in traditional religions that used to define a standard for people. This has left such democracies in a perilous situation of having no clearly defined standard for their citizens. That is why your society has imposed upon you a standard that contains certain contradictions.'

'We have talked about how you grew up in an environment where many people were trying to force a standard upon you from without. We have seen that you resisted this and this caused you to develop a spiral of anger energy. What I want you to see now is that your personal life illustrates what is happening in most modern democracies.'

'Even as a child, you knew intuitively that you were not meant to uncritically accept the standards being forced upon you from without. What you did not see was why this was important for you. The reason was that before you came into this embodiment, you were ready to take the step up to where you begin to take full responsibility for yourself.'

'What exactly does this mean? The uncritical acceptance of an external standard is precisely what enables people to avoid taking responsibility for themselves. How do you take responsibility for yourself? By questioning all of the external standards until you come to the point where your choices are not based on any standard in this world. They come from a higher part of your being.'

'Here is the point I want you to see. Your entire life has been a process of you questioning external standards and resisting the programming from the Machine. Because you did not understand that this served a higher purpose, you reacted

7 | *Freedom from Value Judgments*

with anger. Your anger caused you to be blinded to the very standard that caused your nation to go to war.'

'Even though this led to a harsh consequence, it can still be used in the process of becoming more conscious of who you are and what your life's purpose is. You simply need to acknowledge that you are now at the point in your personal growth process where you are ready to question your standard and reach for a higher way of evaluating choices. My Son, what have you experienced as you were being moved by my words?'

The Warrior looks deeply moved and answers: 'Master, in a few sentences, you have shed an entirely new light on my life. I see now that all those lonely years were so painful only because I did not know that my life has a higher purpose. I see that this was why I could only react with anger. I knew I had to resist being forced, but I did not know why and that made me angry.'

'After I was wounded and started seeing the Machine, I felt I had been misled by my own stupidity into going to war, but I could not admit this consciously because I had no way to do so without condemning myself beyond what I could bear. I was already in so much emotional pain that I could not bear the extra pain of admitting that I had been fooled by the Machine.'

'Master, as you were talking I again went out of my body and I saw this entire mechanism in myself. It was like a living being or beast in my subconscious mind. I also saw that it is not me. I felt like I could let go of it, or at least let go of its hold upon me. I felt like for the first time I could truly disassociate myself from my anger and let it go. After all, everything that happened was simply a step that brought me to where I am today, and I am grateful for being where I am today.'

'My Son, it is precisely such experiences that are the real key to your freedom. Let us use this experience as a launch pad for taking another look at the standard.'

The standard unmasked

'I will now make a statement that will be provocative to many, but I make it because I know you are ready to look at it: *All* of the standards you find in this world are the products of the Machine. They have only one purpose and that is to keep people enslaved by the Machine.'

The Master pauses, sees the perplexed look on the Warrior's face, then says: 'Let me hear your reaction to this statement.'

The Warrior answers: 'I think many people would say that both a society and individuals need to have a standard. I mean, how do we know what is right and wrong behavior unless we have a standard? Wouldn't a society without a standard deteriorate into anarchy or lawlessness where everyone did whatever they wanted and it ended up in chaos?'

The Master says: 'You have brought up the central objection that most people have to my statement. However, I did not say that a society or an individual should have *no* standard at all. I said all of the standards found *in this world* are a product of the Machine. The Machine is so good at producing and camouflaging these standards that most people cannot see any alternative to them. They cannot see that there could be a standard that is *not of this world* and therefore not a product of the Machine. They are so trapped in the Machine that they see no alternative to the Machine.'

The Warrior looks perplexed so the Master continues: 'Take a look at your own story. You went to war because your nation has a standard. Your nation claims to be a nation based on the standard defined by Christ. Yet Christ said to turn the other cheek, to not resist evil and to forgive seventy times seven. How did your nation take this non-violent teaching and turn it into a standard that most of your countrymen believe

7 | Freedom from Value Judgments

justifies that when you are attacked, you do not turn the other cheek but strike back with violence?'

'Based on the fact that you do not follow Christ's call to turn the other cheek, you can see that there is only one answer. Your nation's standard is not based on the teachings of Christ. It is a product of the Machine. What the Machine has done is to take an *unconditional* teaching – turn the other cheek – and turn it into a *conditional* standard. It has taken an *absolute* truth and turned it into a *relative* "truth" that can now seemingly justify something that Christ did not justify.'

The Warrior asks: 'Are you saying my nation should have done nothing when we were attacked?'

The Master replies: 'I am not here going to discuss what your nation should or should not have done. My aim is to help you see the effect of the standard. Your nation was so blinded by the standard defined by the Machine that it could not see and did not seriously consider a non-violent response. In your personal case, you also did not consider a non-violent response. You have personally suffered the return current of what you sent out. I can assure you that your nation also will not escape the return current of what it has projected into the cosmic mirror.'

'Some might say this has already happened, but my deeper purpose here is to help you see that the problem with the standard defined by the Machine is that it is an *external* standard. It is defined by some authority outside yourself, and you have decided to adopt and accept the standard. Most people have accepted the standard of their society without giving it much thought, and certainly without questioning how the standard was defined and whether it is based on untruth or contradictions. You will admit that was the case for you when you went to war?'

When ideas become absolute

The Warrior nods and the Master continues: 'A standard is always defined by raising up certain ideas or statements as being absolute, as having the highest authority, as being beyond questioning. If you do not question these basic paradigms, then you will remain trapped by the standard and your behavior becomes very predictable. You will behave according to the standard. You will find it very difficult to break free from the track upon which your life has been set.'

'In your own case, your life was set on a track from an early age. This caused you to build an anger spiral and you went to war, becoming the perfect killing machine. Had it not been for your severe injury, you would probably still have been trapped by the standard, dedicating your whole life to fighting an external enemy, never even beginning to see the internal enemy that truly keeps you imprisoned.'

'A standard is based on certain axioms that are never questioned. Why are they never questioned? They are supposedly defined by the highest authority, meaning an authority that is far beyond any normal human being. Normal human beings should never question the standard but accept it without reflecting upon its soundness.'

'The acceptance of the standard is always reinforced by penalties. If the standard is defined by a religious authority, it will be claimed that it comes directly from God. If you dare to question it, you will "burn forever in hell." If the standard is defined by a secular authority, it will claim to be based on the undeniable facts of science, on historical necessity or other means. In any case, there can be penalties imposed by society, or there may be the penalty that you will be excluded from your local community. What is the standard based on? It is based on a part of the mind that is normally called the intellect

7 | *Freedom from Value Judgments* 97

or the analytical mind. What is analytical thinking? It is comparative thinking. This can be illustrated by a computer. When it receives new input, the computer compares it to its existing database. It looks for something in its database that is similar to the new input. When it has found this, it uses its predefined content and programming to determine its response to the input.'

How people become biological robots

'The most subtle and unnoticed effect of the Machine is that it makes most human beings function as a kind of biological robots. When you went to war, you were not truly thinking; you were not thinking *creatively*.'

'When your nation was attacked and your leader called for those who would fight the enemy, your mind functioned like a computer. You compared the new input to your database, which was heavily influenced by your personal anger spiral and by your upbringing in a society based on a contradictory standard. You found it easy to decide to go to war. From that moment on, all of your decisions were within the framework defined by your nation's military. You never questioned your standard until you were injured and went outside the cloud in which your mind had been trapped.'

'The intellect is a useful faculty for performing many tasks in your practical life. The intellect is a tool and as with any tool, it is wise to know its limitations. The main limitation of the intellect is that it can never question its database. To the intellect, the database is beyond questioning. The intellect can only compare new input to its database. If the new input does not fit with what is in the database, then the intellect will always reason that the new input is wrong. The intellect will never question the database. This is not to say that people cannot question their databases. This cannot be done by the intellect with its comparative thinking. It can only be done by a higher part of the mind that is able to think creatively. The main effect of the Machine is to cause people to refuse to use this faculty. They may even be ignorant of the fact that they have the ability to think creatively. Many live their entire lives without having a truly creative thought. All of their thoughts and actions are predetermined by the Machine.'

Why people fight each other

'Let us again look at your personal experience. The enemy attacked your nation. You went to war and felt that your killing of the enemy was completely justified according to your nation's standard. Let us now go to the other side and look at the thinking of your enemy. You will see that your enemies also felt that their violence against your nation was completely justified by *their* standard.'

'What you see now is an example of two groups of people who each have a standard. Each group feels that their standard is the only right one because it is based on an unquestionable authority. That is why each group feels justified in taking the radical step of killing other human beings in order to defend their standard.'

'Each group is absolutely convinced that its standard and its way of life is the ultimate one. The only outcome of the conflict that they can see is that their group is victorious by eradicating the standard of the other group—possibly eradicating all people who follow this standard if necessary. The standard is an abstract idea but human beings are very physical

7 | Freedom from Value Judgments

and very alive. What sense does it make to kill a *living* human being in order to preserve an already *dead* idea?'

'My Son, what I hope you can begin to see here is that both of these standards are created by the Machine. They have only one purpose, namely to keep people enslaved by the Machine. The Machine accomplishes this by defining different standards for different groups. The standards are defined in such a way that there will be an inevitable and unresolvable conflict between the two groups. The Machine does this partly because it is itself based on an unresolvable contradiction, but it also does it because it can survive only by people feeding it energy. The primary way that people feed energy to the Machine is through conflicts and strife.'

'The false standards of this world all define differences between categories of people and then apply a value judgment, saying some human beings are less human than others. The real "standard" is based on the fact that all life is one. All people are of equal value and deserve equal respect.'

'Can you begin to see that any time – *any* time – two groups are in conflict, it is because each group is blinded by the Machine? Each group is looking at the situation through a perception filter. Each group thinks their perception filter is based on an absolute authority, but in reality it is based on a relative argument that is defined by the Machine and presented as having ultimate authority. Do you begin to see this?'

The Warrior thinks for a long time, then says: 'Master, I think I understand this at the level of the mind, but I do not truly "see" it and I know you want me to go beyond understanding.'

The Master says: 'Good, you are becoming honest. I admit this is difficult to see. I will give you a few more teachings then ask you to do some exercises for clearing the level of your mind that is beyond the mental level, namely your sense of identity.'

'What I want you to consider as you perform these exercises is that the standard defined by the Machine is imposed upon you from outside yourself, from outside the core of your being. In your identity body, you will find two "selves." One is the self you have built as you grew up. It is very much relative to your outer situation, your family and society. This is who the world – and therefore also the Machine – wants you to be. When you go beyond this outer identity, you will discover the core of your being.'

'You have already had direct experiences of a state of mind in which you were not looking at the world through the perception filter of the outer self. Because of this, you are far ahead of most people. If a person has not had such an experience, it is very difficult to question and free oneself from the outer self.'

Finding truth within yourself

'What I want you to ponder is how the standard imposed from without keeps you from going within and questioning the outer standard. It keeps you from exercising the central human capability, namely the ability to know truth by contacting a higher source within yourself.'

'Right now, humankind is faced with the challenge of going beyond the relative standards defined by the Machine. This is brought about partly by overall cycles and partly by the development of technology. If humankind does not find a peaceful way to resolve conflict, then the ever-increasing destructive capacity of modern weapons will lead to a planetary disaster.'

'Many people are ready to take this step. The only way to do it is to do what you have done, namely look inside yourself.

7 | Freedom from Value Judgments

You must be willing to face the false self. Only by seeing the beam in your own eye, will you be able to find the true self. Only when enough people find their true selves – and thereby find a standard that is not defined by the Machine – will a peaceful resolution to conflict be possible.'

'When I talk about a resolution to conflict, I am not talking about one worldly standard eradicating another. I am talking about people transcending the consciousness that caused them to think there was a real conflict. This is caused by the realization that both of the conflicting standards are unreal.'

'In your case, I want you to ponder the mindset you were in as you went to war. Can you remember how you looked at the enemy in those days?'

The Warrior says: 'Well, I looked at them as the bad guys, as the ones who hated us and would destroy our nation if they could.'

The Master says: 'Yes, but I want you to think deeper. Let me help you. You have told me that you were able to kill a person from the enemy's side without reflecting upon it. Would you have been able to kill a person from your own side?'

'Of course not!'

'Why not? My Son, consider this statement: "No human being can kill another human being." Did you truly see the enemy as human beings, as individuals like yourself?'

The Warrior replies: 'Master, I never even thought of that before. You are right, I didn't actually look at the enemy as being humans like myself. I didn't consider them to be individuals with fathers and mothers and sisters and brothers who would miss them when I killed them. So you are right, if I had looked at them as human beings like myself, I would not have been able to kill them. This is amazing. Are you saying the Machine made me unable to see the enemy as human beings and that is why I was able to kill them?'

'Yes,' the Master replies, 'the effect of the Machine is to make people forget the universal core of their beings. This is the universal nature that all people share, the bond that is beyond all of the divisions found in this world. People begin to see themselves as separate from those of another group. Those separate beings "over there" are not truly human like themselves. That is why it becomes possible to kill them. One human being cannot kill another human being, but when the others are not seen as quite as human as yourself, then killing becomes possible.'

'What you had done was to build a self or a sense of identity as being a warrior. This self did not exist in your mental body; it existed in your identity body. The warrior self controlled your thinking. It caused you to see yourself as a separate being and the enemy as other separate beings. All of your thinking revolved around how you could defeat and kill the enemy. Your thoughts stayed within the framework defined by your warrior self and that is why you never questioned the justification for killing. How can the mental body of a warrior question the need to kill when that need is defined at the higher level of the identity body?'

'As you perform the exercises for clearing your identity body, I want you to watch for the separate self and how it will very cleverly seek to defend your identity as a separate being. I also want you to watch for the unified self, the core of your being. The separate self is based on the illusion that reality can be divided into separate compartments. The true self is based on the hidden reality that all life is one. When you truly see that all life is one, your victory over the Machine will be won.'

8 | THE SEVEN BEASTS

Time passes. One day, after the usual practices in the assembly hall, the Master asks the Warrior to tell him about his experiences.

The Warrior replies: 'Master, this was the most difficult experience yet. It seems like the outer self is very good at hiding itself, almost like a chameleon. After having invoked light and my mind feeling clear, I would sometimes get a glimpse, almost like a creature moving in the forest but always behind the leaves so I could not see it. It was a shadow or a form moving, but no clear vision of what it was.'

The bear

'This went on for a long time, but one day I finally had a clear vision. I saw myself walking in the woods and came across a huge bear standing on all fours, eating berries from some bushes. At first, it seemed very peaceful and friendly, barely noticing me, but then it suddenly reared up on its hind legs and roared at me with a sound so powerful it made my blood freeze. I felt like the energy coming from the bear was paralyzing me and I could not move. I was so shocked I came out of the meditation and the vision disappeared. What does this mean, Master?'

'My Son, you have encountered one of the internal spirits or beasts that make up your separate self. Over time, many people have seen these, sometimes as animals, sometimes as mythological creatures. The story of Odysseus can be read as a journey into his subconscious mind where he encountered and overcame the various creatures hiding in his own mind. This is a journey all of us must make, at least if we want to be free from the Machine.'

'Think about the behavior of the bear. It is first peaceful but then suddenly roars at you with no apparent provocation. Is there a person in your life that this reminds you of?'

The Warrior answers: 'Yes, it reminds me of my father. He would seem quite normal most of the time, but sometimes he would fly into this rage and there was no way you could reason with him. You simply had to get out of the way. There was no way to tell when this would happen, which made it all the more scary because you just didn't know how to avoid it so you were always on guard.'

The Master says: 'Good. In recognizing your father's behavior, what did you do in order to deal with this?'

'Oh, I see,' the Warrior replies, 'I actually took on the same pattern. I can also sometimes feel so overwhelmed with anger energy that I fly into a rage. This is how I was all the time when you met me in the marketplace, but I have had the tendency all of my life. While I was at war, I would often go into this rage when in battle and would kill the enemy blindly, even if they were not a direct threat. So you are saying the bear represents not only my father's anger but my own as well?'

8 | The Seven Beasts

The Master says: 'It also represents the anger in all of us. There is a huge bear-like beast in the collective unconscious. Most people have a miniature bear in their own energy fields. It is through this personal bear that they are controlled by the Machine because the personal beast becomes an open door for the collective one.'

'What you have seen now is that you took on the same behavior pattern that you saw in your father. This is what we all do. As small children we are imitators. We take on whatever behavior we see in the adults around us, even what we get from movies and books. You can look at your own parents and if they have a certain obvious trait, you will have the same in yourself.'

'Here is where it gets tricky. In many cases, people are not aware that they have the same kind of behavior as that of a parent. This is the case when the parent was clearly unbalanced and abusive. If the child experienced the parent as doing something clearly wrong, then the child not only took on the same pattern, it also created another beast to deal with the parent's behavior.'

'This is a reactionary beast. It is based on seeing the parent's behavior as wrong, thereby judging that this is something you do not want to do. This reactionary beast has two functions. It helps you deal with your parent's behavior when you are a child and thus not able to resist or remove yourself. As an adult, the beast helps you limit the other beast so people, in most cases, do not do what their parents did, or they don't do it to the same degree.'

'The problem is that this also makes people think that they do not have the same tendency as their parents. The second beast hides the presence of the first beast and both beasts are hidden in the subconscious. This makes it possible for people to deny that they sometimes do what their parents did. The second beast can also make you very judgmental towards other people or towards yourself. You are very condemning of behavior that resembles that of your parents.'

'Some people would say the second beast is helpful because it limits abusive behavior. This is only because they don't realize that it is also tied to a beast in the collective unconscious. The Machine can use both beasts to control you. Do you remember what I said a long time ago, namely that whether you submit to the Machine or rebel against the Machine, you are still controlled by the Machine? You need to uncover and undo each of the two beasts that are created as a pair. Only by seeing and consciously dismissing both of them will you be free. The Machine has nothing in you in that area.'

'Here is what I want you to do. I want you to invoke light into consuming the anger energies of the bear. Even the very thoughtform of the bear. After each time you do this, I want you to watch out for the second beast that you created in order to react to the bear in your father.'

The raven

Time passes, and the Master again asks the Warrior to describe his experiences. The Warrior replies: 'This was amazing, Master. It was really difficult to consume the thoughtform of the bear. It took a lot of work, and it was as if I simply could not see beyond the bear to see the second beast. It just kept hiding itself from me.'

'One day I saw the vision of a bear eating from the carcass of a moose and around it were all these ravens. The bear would seem peaceful, but suddenly it would lash out at the ravens. I noticed that they were always watching the bear and keeping a distance so they could move away if the bear lashed out. I then started thinking about what the raven represents and how it has often been a symbol of death.'

'After continuing to invoke light to consume the energy of the bear, I one day saw a vision of the bear lying dead in the snow. Around and on top of it were all these ravens, and one of them was hacking at the eyes of the bear. In a flash, I saw that this was the beast I had built in reaction to my father's bear behavior. I was powerless to stop or resist the bear so I simply had to be always watchful and ready to get out of the way. At the same time, I was thinking that this would not last forever, just like a raven sitting in a tree waiting for a wounded animal to die.'

'The thought came to me: "You have power over me now, but one day, you'll be dead and then I'll hack your eyes out!" I was really shocked but realized this is how I felt about my father being abusive when I was a child. Of course, I then started invoking light to consume the energies and thoughtform of the raven. After a lot of work, I one day had a vision of standing on top of a mountain and above me was a clear, blue sky. I looked all around and noticed there were no ravens in the sky, but high above me an eagle soared.'

The Master says: 'This is a good result. You have cleared away both of the spirits, the aggressive bear and the reactionary, but still vengeful, raven. Can you see that there is also anger in the thoughtform of the raven? It is simply waiting for the bear to die and then it will hack the eyes out as an act of revenge that springs from anger?'

The Warrior replies: 'Yes, I realized the raven carries a lot of silent, inner rage, and I can see that in myself also. I see how I built this inner rage by having to submit to my father. When I was at war, I took it out on the enemy. In a sense, the raven represents the anger that patiently waits for an opportunity to strike back, and when it comes, the raven is transformed into the bear at its worst.'

'When it is waiting, the raven is mocking the bear and thinking it is wiser because it is so patient and seemingly not aggressive. Yet the raven cannot hunt for itself and needs the scraps of the carcasses killed by the bear. It is like it feeds off the energy of the bear.'

'Very good observation,' the Master replies. 'The two beasts or spirits are created as a pair, meaning they are co-dependent upon each other. Sometimes the ravens have found a carcass and as they circle it, the bear becomes aware of its position. The bear also feels more powerful when it sees the ravens flee from its assaults. One cannot exist without the other, but *you* can exist without both.'

'This brings me to your vision that when you had dissolved both of the beasts that form a pair, you saw the eagle soaring. The soaring eagle is a symbol for your real self, what I call the Conscious You, when it has realized that it is neither of the two beasts or spirits. When you see that you are neither this beast nor that beast, you will not be pulled into struggling as the beasts do. When you stop resisting, you can spread your wings and glide on the upward energy currents of the cosmos. You will then rise effortlessly, and the view of the eagle from above is greater than the view from any mountain top on earth.'

'While this is a great victory for you, you are not yet ready to soar into the sky. That is why you saw the eagle above you instead of seeing yourself as the eagle.'

'There are innumerable beasts that humankind has created over the ages. You do not personally have all of them; each person has his or her individual combination, all of which must be cleared before you are free from the Machine.'

The seven pairs

'There are seven pairs of beasts that are common to all people. I have told you that everything is energy. Your physical body is not made from solid matter; it is truly made from vibrating energy. Obviously, your body is not made from the flowing energy that we know as electricity or sunlight; it is made from energy that has temporarily been captured into a stationary field, an energy matrix. Your body is truly an energy field.'

'There are some teachings that compare your body to a magnet. You know that a magnet has an invisible field around it. Some say your physical body also has an invisible energy field around it. This is technically true, but the problem is that in saying the body has a field around it, you imply that the body produces the energy field as a magnet is said to produce the magnetic field. In reality this is neither correct for the body nor the magnet.'

'The higher understanding is that everything that appears in the macroscopic world of "solid" matter is like the tip of an iceberg. Ninety percent of the iceberg is under the surface of the water. Likewise, your physical body is the most dense part of your total energy field, what I have called the four levels of your mind, or the four lower bodies.'

'This energy field is the vehicle that the Conscious You is using in order to experience the macroscopic world and in order to express its creative powers in this world. You are truly a co-creative being, sent here in order to help co-create the world started by your spiritual parents.'

'You co-create by directing a stream of creative energy, and this energy flows through your total energy field. This field has seven major energy centers or portals, often called chakras.

Each chakra acts as a valve that can open or close. Each chakra can be the open door for letting through one of the seven creative energies that make up our universe. When all of your chakras are cleared, you have maximum creative powers.'

'The major effect of the Machine is that it has caused most people to close all of their chakras almost completely. The chakras are no longer the open doors for the creative energies to stream into this world. They are only letting in a very small portion of light.'

'The process of closing the chakras happens as you are attacked by an aggressive spirit and then create a reactionary spirit in order to deal with this attack. This sets up an action-reaction pattern. The passive spirit causes you to suppress the light by closing the valve in a chakra. This builds tension, and once in a while the aggressive spirit takes over. Light is now flowing through the chakra, but it is instantly misqualified with a fear-based vibration.'

'It is this fear-based energy that has created and which feeds the Machine. You are turned into a cow that can be milked for energy by the Machine. You are like a cow standing in the barn and hooked up to one of these milking machines. At any time, the machine can turn on by causing you to have to react to some provocation from without. You immediately go into one of your action-reaction patterns, and this produces fear-based energy that is milked by the Machine.'

'The Machine survives by getting you to reduce the love-based energy so it cannot flow through your chakras at full force. The reduced flow is then turned into fear-based energy that feeds the Machine. The Machine needs you to reduce the flow of love-based energy because a free flow of this energy will liberate you from the influence of the Machine. It will also help remove the darkness from the world, which will eventually help all people see the Machine and free themselves from it.

8 | The Seven Beasts

The survival of the Machine depends on getting you to reduce the flow of love-based energy while getting you to turn what is flowing into fear-based energy. A full flow of love-based energy would prevent you from being fooled by the illusions of the Machine, the illusions that make it seem necessary to react with fear.'

'You, my Son, have engaged in the process of freeing yourself from the Machine by confronting and rising above the spirit pairs in your seven chakras. All people who wish to be free from the Machine must do the same. All people must clear the chakras, but not in the same order.'

'In your case, you started by seeing the bear and the raven because that is the chakra with the greatest perversion. You will next go to the chakra with the second-largest accumulation of fear-based energy, but the order will be different for each person. Even the animals that symbolize each chakra can vary from culture to culture, person to person.'

'The bear and the raven correspond to the chakra that is located over the solar plexus area. This chakra corresponds to the sixth spiritual ray. The Alpha quality of this ray is peace and the Omega quality is service. The main perversion of the ray of peace is to be a warrior who claims to be fighting for peace. You are seeking to create peace by killing all those who are different from you. You claim to be serving some greater cause by killing other human beings.'

'My students will help you learn special exercises for invoking the love-based energies of the ray of peace to consume all remnants of anti-peace in your energy field. After you have done this, you will no doubt have a vision of the next animal that comes up, and we will talk about the meaning of this.'

'Master,' the Warrior asks, 'I am wondering about the bear and the raven. I know some native medicine men and shamans use the bear and the raven and other animals to symbolize positive qualities. You seem to be using them to symbolize the perversions?'

'My Son, I am not saying there is an actual bear or a raven in your energy field. They are only used as symbols because dreams and visions often attempt to show us something in the form of symbols. They must use symbols that are familiar to us.'

'All symbols can be used and interpreted in different ways by different cultures, and this is perfectly acceptable. I use them in one way and I have no problem with someone else using them in a different way. I have no intention of saying that my use of symbols is the only right one and all others are wrong.'

'Each teacher must teach within his or her own context. What many shamans and medicine men teach is perfectly valid within their context. What I teach is valid only within my own context. The point for a student is to avoid going into the mindset of wanting to elevate one teaching to the superior one. This form of competition or exclusiveness comes from and feeds the Machine.'

'It is important for a student to approach teachings from the viewpoint of what works for the individual at his or her present stage of the path. If what another teacher teaches works for you, then by all means make the best of that teaching. My teaching works, but only if you go into and accept my context, my world view. If people cannot do that, I hope they find another teacher that works for them. There are many ways to become trapped by the Machine. For each way of becoming trapped, there is a teaching that can help you free yourself from the clutches of the Machine.'

9 | THE LION AND THE SNAKE

After some time, the Warrior tells the master that he has had a vision of another animal: 'Master, I have now several times in meditation seen a male lion. He is very energetic and aggressive in defending his territory, roaring at me if I get too close. His roar is even louder and more frightening than the roar of the bear. Sometimes, he just lies there, looking over his territory as if at peace, but without any visible provocation, he can start roaring or attack anything that moves. What does the lion symbolize?'

The Master replies: 'Strange as it may seem, the male lion symbolizes the third spiritual ray. This is the ray of love. This may be hard to see at first, but the third ray corresponds to the chakra that is located at the same height as the physical heart but in the center of the chest. You will know that the lion has also been used to symbolize courage and some warriors have been said to have the heart of a lion.'

'The male lion has been called the king of the beasts because of his regal appearance and manner. He is fiercely territorial and will attack anyone who seems to threaten his claim to ownership. This is much like the kings, emperors and dictators seen throughout history who will also kill anyone threatening their claim of ownership.'

'The sense of ownership or possessiveness is one of the primary perversions of love. Look how many people claim that they love another person, but then they feel entitled to act as if they own the object of their love. Much of what people call love relationships are sophisticated games of seeking to own or control other people. This is most clearly seen in a love-hate relationship where a person can instantly shift from claiming to love another to now openly expressing hatred for the same person. If the object of "love" refuses to be controlled, then the person who claims to love can quickly develop an intent of destroying the other person.'

'This possessive love shows that such people truly do not love. They are playing a game of control. The person they say they love is an "object of love." The person is an object, not a real, independent human being. The person who loves possessively has no respect for the other person's free will and right to self-determination. The "loved" person should behave as an object that can be owned and controlled. When the person refuses to be objectified, the person who claims to love will now seek to destroy the beloved as easily as you destroy an object.'

'You will see, my Son, that you had also objectified the enemy and did not see him as a real person that deserved respect. You killed the enemy as easily as you destroyed a non-living object.'

'This is a perversion of love, and all warriors have this as a prominent element of the subconscious. Of course, all of the people in your nation who supported the war also have taken in this perversion of love. Otherwise, they would have demonstrated in order to stop your leader from going to war. I will have my other students teach you how to invoke the positive light of the third ray of love.'

The snake

'I want you to take a closer look at your vision of the male lion standing on a cliff, looking over his territory. I want you to look for the other animal that you did not notice.'

The Warrior looks confused and says: 'Master, I did not see any other animal in my vision. I noticed only the lion.'

The Master tells the Warrior to close his eyes and focus on the vision of the lion. He then says: 'My Son, look down upon the cliff where the lion is standing. There is another animal that is almost invisible in the grass.'

Suddenly, the Warrior almost jumps in his seat: 'Master, as I was looking, I suddenly saw a snake, and the moment I saw it, it lashed out at me with its venomous fangs. It almost scared me out of my body.'

'Good,' says the Master, 'you have now seen the companion to the lion. The snake or serpent represents another perversion of the heart chakra.'

'Your energy field is being upheld by a constant stream of spiritual energy from your higher self. As this energy descends into your field, it first enters the heart chakra from where it is distributed to all of the other chakras. This means that the perversions that are in the heart chakra will color the light before it reaches the other chakras. That is why some people are said to have an evil heart.'

'Consider the important symbolical story of the Garden of Eden. This story symbolizes the process that all people have gone through. In the distant past, you lived in an edenic environment. You were able to manifest everything you needed for your sustenance by using the co-creative powers of your mind. You did this by working with the "God" in the garden, which is actually a symbol for your higher self and your spiritual teachers in a higher realm.'

'There is no necessity of you leaving this edenic state, but because you have free will, leaving paradise is a possibility. How do you leave paradise? By falling prey to the temptation represented by the serpent. The serpent said to Eve (who was not a woman but a symbol for the feminine aspect, the soul, of every human being) that she could become "as a God, knowing good and evil."'

'This symbolizes that you have two options for experimenting with your creative abilities. One is to remain aware that you are not a God, you are a co-creator with God. You acknowledge a reality outside your own mind and perception filter.'

Acting like a God

'The other option is to go into a frame of mind in which you see yourself as a separate being. You now fall prey to the temptation of the serpent, namely to set yourself up as a God who can define what is good and evil. You do not acknowledge any reality outside your own perception filter. You think that what you see through the perception filter is the only reality. Instead of an outside authority defining reality, you have now become the God who defines reality.'

'This tendency to make yourself a God is what created the Machine. As long as people are trapped in this mindset, they will be manipulated by the Machine, they will be the slaves of the Machine. Jesus called the Machine the "prince of this world" and the Buddha called it "Maya."'

'When you think that you are the God defining good and evil, your heart chakra will be colored by your definition. The light coming from your higher self is colored from the very beginning. None of the other chakras can question or go beyond the coloring in the heart. What the heart chakra is full of, the other chakras overflow with.'

'Clearing the heart chakra is essential for those who want to be free from the Machine. It may be easy to see the lion, but the serpent is more subtil than all of the other animals. The essence of the serpent's mindset is that the end can justify the means. The serpent defines a goal of epic importance that must be reached. Then is says that any means necessary are justified by the importance of the goal.'

'We earlier talked about how your nation could go to war while claiming to be a religious nation based on the teaching "Thou shallt not kill." The explanation is that your nation, both its people and its leaders, have been deceived by the serpentine logic.'

'A goal has been defined. It has been set up as being of epic importance to attain this goal. If the goal *is not* attained, the worst possible calamity will come to pass for all people and the earth as a whole. If the goal *is* achieved, the highest possible reward will come to those who help attain the goal. The unconditional teaching "Thou shallt not kill" has now been made conditional. Because the enemy is opposing the epic goal, it is justified that you kill the enemy. The very same God who told you not to kill, will give you a reward for killing the enemy.'

'My Son, for many people the heart chakra will be the last one that they clear because of the subtleties of the serpentine mind. In your case, it is the second one because you do have great courage. While you were in battle, you did have the heart of a lion and that is why you risked your own life to help a wounded comrade. There is symbolic importance to the fact that it was your courageous heart that caused you to be wounded and thus set you on a different course that leads towards your freedom from the Machine.'

'My other students will now guide you to the exercises for clearing the heart chakra and invoking the unconditional love energies of the third spiritual ray. This will help you clear the energies of both the lion and the serpent, and then we will see which animal comes up next.'

10 | THE WOLF AND THE CARIBOU

Later, the Warrior tells the Master that he has had a vision of a wolf hunting a caribou. The Master explains: 'The wolf symbolizes the chakra that is located over the throat. This chakra corresponds to the first spiritual ray that is characterized by power and will.'

'For you, it is natural that this comes up because as a warrior you have to be able to use power and you must have a strong will. In battle, your will to live may be all that keeps you alive. Unfortunately, your will to live easily becomes perverted into a will to kill. You think your survival depends on killing the enemy before he kills you. This now becomes a will to kill without reflection upon the necessity of killing. Killing becomes almost a reflex.'

'The wolf symbolizes this because when it hunts the caribou, it is incapable of reflecting on the necessity of killing. It also shows no mercy or consideration for the suffering of the caribou; although it also has no desire to deliberately harm or torture the caribou.'

'The throat chakra is what determines people's use of power. In most people, the Machine has caused them to close their power center so they have very little will or power to act. This is symbolized by the caribou, which is not only a victim of the wolf but is a heard animal. Many people have very little individual will but follow the crowd in everything from choice of career to what they wear. This is the result of shutting off your individual will power.'

'Other people have opened up for a flow of energy through their power center, but the Machine has caused them to express it through force. There is a subtle but all-important difference between power and force. It is perfectly possible to express power without forcing other people.'

'The two characteristics of the first ray are power and will. You must have will before you can create anything. You must exercise power in order to manifest what you will to create. These are essential and positive qualities. It is perfectly possible for you to exercise will and power without force. Before people entered the serpentine consciousness, they exercised will and power with the awareness that they were part of a larger whole. Their will and power were in harmony with the overall purpose of raising the whole.'

'The Machine needs you to exercise power and will in a perverted way. This happens when you go into the illusion that you are a separate being. If everyone is seeking to raise the whole, there is no competition or conflict between people. When they go into separation, they become focused on raising themselves in comparison to others. There is now a constant struggle between people. One person sees that the will of other people is in contradiction to his own will. He thinks that the only way for him to manifest his own will is to force the will of other people. They must be forced to submit. This is how a dictator is born, but there are dictators everywhere, from families to corporations. The misuse of power has divided humankind into two groupings, namely those who have perverted their will and seek to dominate through force and those who have shut down their will and have submitted to dominance. They are now following the heard, which is being herded by the wolf pack into the desired position for the kill.'

'Sometimes the wolves create panic in the heard, as you see for example when the stock market takes a downturn or the event that caused your nation to go to war. This is all staged in order to get people to submit and to get them to release fear-based energy that feeds the Machine. The wolves think they gain power from this, and they do. The price they pay is that even though they have the power to control the heard, they have given their power to the Machine. Those who control others are themselves controlled by the Machine.'

'You have started freeing yourself from the Machine, and this involves purifying your will and power. You must have the will to be free, but this is not the same as the will to rebel against he machine. You will never be free by rebelling. Your will must be purified so that it is completely directed at a positive, life-supporting purpose. As you purify your throat chakra and the other chakras, you will realize that you do not need to use force in order to be free from the Machine.'

'The Machine has trapped you through force. It may seem as if the only way to be free is to use so much force that you break the bonds the Machine has used to tie you. The more force you use, the more you reinforce the bonds for they are created from force-based energy.'

'The only way to become free from the Machine is to stop using force and to learn how to use will and power without force. This is why the Great Master told us not to resist evil but to turn the other cheek. If your nation had been willing to learn that lesson, you would not have been sent to war.

Of course, given your own eagerness to go to war, how could a nation learn a lesson when its individual citizens had not learned that lesson? What is a nation but the sum of the minds of its citizens?'

'Again, my other students will show you exercises for clearing the throat chakra. As you do so, the next animal will emerge from the mists of the subconscious swampland. As the mist over the bog clears, who knows what creatures become visible?'

The Warrior says: 'Master, I have a feeling you already know what will show up next.'

The Master replies: 'Perhaps, but the value for you is that you experience it for yourself so that it has the greatest possible impact and gives you the drive to work through it.'

11 | THE SEA MONSTER AND THE JELLY FISH

Some time later, the Warrior tells the Master that he has encountered the next animal pair: 'Master, after having worked hard on clearing the energies in the throat chakra, I had another vision. I saw myself riding with my father in a motor boat. The sea was completely calm, like glass. Suddenly, this huge sea monster raised its head above the water. It was one of these dinosaurs with a long neck and small head, like the Loch Ness monster.'

'Strangely, I was completely calm inside and slowly raised my army rifle and shot it several times in the neck. It shivered and then sank beneath the surface. Where it disappeared, a lot of waves came up and then thousands of jelly fish became visible in the water.'

The Master comments: 'My Son, you have now encountered the animal pair that symbolizes the chakra that is located on top of the head. This is often called the crown chakra, and its symbol is the lotus flower. The chakra is also called the "thousand-petaled lotus." This explains why this chakra is symbolized by water animals. The lotus blossom grows from the bottom of the mud up through the murky water only to produce one of the most beautiful flowers. All kinds of creatures can hide in the murky water of the subconscious.'

'The crown chakra is the opening for the energies of the second spiritual ray. It is associated with wisdom or the ability to discern what is real and unreal.'

'The sea monster represents the Alpha or aggressive aspect of a perversion of wisdom. This is when you have fallen prey to the serpentine illusion and you think you know everything. You have then become a predator that swims through the collective consciousness, seeking to destroy any idea or thought system that contradicts or goes beyond your own. There is much of this going on in academic circles, in religion, in politics and in the media.'

'Many people have become dominated by this sea monster energy and think they are the superior rulers of the collective consciousness. The majority of the population have become followers of these self-proclaimed leaders, and this is represented by the jelly fish. Although a jelly fish can swim, it cannot go against the strong currents flowing through the ocean. These currents are generated by the wake of the sea monsters as they swim through the waters. The jelly fish are helplessly swept along.'

'The challenge of clearing the crown chakra is delicate. You need to invoke wisdom, but it is not human, intellectual or worldly wisdom. The aggressive leaders will claim that a human being does not have the ability to know wisdom on its own. In this, they are correct in the sense that you cannot know true wisdom through the human mind or ego.'

'What the aggressive leaders do not see is that this applies to themselves as well. They think they are exceptions. They claim they can know wisdom and that the population should

11 | The Sea Monster and the Jelly Fish

accept their superiority and follow them. They think they have a right, even a duty, to destroy all other thought systems that claim to have ultimate wisdom. If some of the delicate jelly fish become shattered by the turbulence, the leaders think this is simply the price that must be paid in order to create decisive results. This is certainly true for those who in their perverted wisdom sent your nation to war.'

'The "wisdom" defined by these false leaders is a relative or dualistic wisdom. It is based on a one-sided view of an issue. It is the serpentine wisdom that defines an epic goal and then it defines the means for achieving the goal as justified. When the ends can justify the means – especially the means of killing people – you know you are dealing with perverted wisdom.'

'The challenge is to realize that while you cannot have true wisdom through the outer mind, the intellect and the ego, you can have it by going within. What I call the Conscious You can step outside the perception filter of the outer mind, and then you can have a direct experience of true wisdom. The challenge is that this wisdom cannot easily be expressed in words. It is a totality that can only be fully known through direct experience.'

'As a teacher, I cannot give you the fullness of wisdom through words. I can only do so by taking you to the point where you experience the totality of the Spirit of Wisdom, namely those ascended masters who embody the second ray and the other rays.'

'Your experience of the sea monster and the jelly fish is significant. Your father being in the boat with you shows that you are still seeking to navigate the waters of your own subconscious through the vehicle that he built. The fact that you remained calm when you encountered the sea monster shows you have started to free yourself. The fact that you shot the sea monster shows you are still not free from the tendency to respond with force. My other students will teach you how to invoke the energies of the second ray of wisdom. We will teach you that you do not overcome the aggressive beast through force but by letting it be consumed by spiritual fire.'

'In your case, you are not dominated by the jelly fish energy, but in the army you did in a sense have to become like a jelly fish. You had to take orders and you were not allowed to think for yourself. You had to follow procedures thought out by others and were not allowed to question them. I understand that some will say this is necessary for soldiers, but it is only necessary in situations where you go to war. Such situations are not necessary from a wider perspective.'

'There are some people who see themselves as leaders, and they may appear powerful among men. In reality, their minds have been completely taken over by the serpentine logic that drives the Machine. These leaders appear as sea monsters and they feel powerful when they swim among the jelly fish of the general population. They feel how they can easily create a current that sweeps most people along, and it makes them feel powerful. In reality, they are also helplessly swept along by the currents generated by the Machine. They simply don't feel the larger currents that move them. Even a powerful sea monster is swept along by the Gulf Stream.'

'In order to be free from the Machine, you cannot be a jelly fish, but neither can you be a sea monster or one who resists the sea monster. You must find the Middle Way between not submitting to force and not rebelling by using force. True power is beyond force. When you clear all of your chakras, you will begin to have true creative power. You will then naturally begin to find the Middle Way that is above and beyond both dualistic polarities. It is beyond what the Buddha called "the pairs."'

12 | THE HAWK AND THE SPIDER

One day, the Warrior tells the Master: 'I have now had a dream several times where I see a hawk flying through the forest, always looking for prey. A couple of times, it has flown between the branches of trees only to be caught in a giant net made by a spider. As the hawk struggled helplessly in the net and the spider came closer and closer, I would awaken bathed in sweat and with great fear. What does this dream signify?'

'My Son, it shows that you are now working on clearing the chakra that is located at the brow, midway between the physical eyes. It is the chakra that relates to vision. This is not physical vision but *non-physical* vision.'

'This non-physical vision can relate to being able to see or sense what is beyond the material world. For example, some people can see the human energy field with its chakras. Others can see non-physical creatures, which can be a very disturbing experience. Many overlook that vision also relates to how you perceive the world; the mental images you hold in your mind.

Vision is not just a passive quality of opening your eyes and seeing whatever comes to you. It is very much an active quality of forming mental images and projecting them upon other people and the world.'

'Whenever people seek to control others, be it through physical force or psychic force, they have perverted vision. As a soldier in war, your entire reason for being a soldier is based on a perverted vision. As we have talked about before, you do not see the enemy as being humans, at least not as you see yourself. You have created a mental image that portrays the enemy as being subhumans, or you have created an image that says it is justifiable to kill the enemy in order to further a necessary cause. Anything that justifies the use of force is perverted vision. Anything that divides human beings into categories that can be treated differently is perverted vision.'

'The hawk is only one among several animals that can symbolize the brow or third-eye chakra. In your culture, you have the concept of having a hawk-eye. The symbol is that the hawk is always looking for weaknesses, as a soldier is always looking for weaknesses in the enemy. You are looking for weaknesses in the enemy's tactic, strategy, weapons and position so that you might defeat him.'

'Beyond that, you have created a mental image and projected it upon the enemy. This image is entirely negative. It portrays the enemy as a being who can only be wrong and yourself as a being who can only be right.'

'Many, many people have been trapped in such a one-sided perception for a very long time. You were trapped in it for years. Even though you saw things that you knew did not conform to your vision, you were able to ignore or deny them until you were wounded yourself.'

'What you experienced when you were lying wounded in the desert was the situation of the hawk who has been caught in the net of the spider. You realize you are trapped and you struggle against it. The more you struggle, the more you become enveloped in the sticky strands of the net. Eventually, you are immobilized and can only wait for the spider to approach you and suck out your insides.'

'The spider represents the passive perversion of vision. The hawk is the active and a hawk can have a great sense of freedom. It is free to fly through the forest and can spot the slightest movement and avoid the dense thickets. Yet it cannot avoid what it cannot see, and it cannot see the net spun by the spider.'

'The trickiness of perverted vision is that it is based on a partial or one-sided perception. This perception filter blocks out certain aspects of reality so you do not see them or do not see them as real. This has an inevitable side-effect, namely that you spin a net of what some spiritual philosophies call karma.'

'Karma is unbalanced action and it comes from unbalanced vision. Precisely because your perception blocks out certain aspects of reality – such as the fact that all people are created with equal rights and value – you spin a net of karma, which is made by threads of energy. The very filter that forms the basis for you creating the net also makes it impossible to see the net. If you could see that your vision was unbalanced, you would correct it and therefore not create the net.'

'The inevitable consequence – which no one can avoid no matter how much they deny this reality – is that sooner or later, you will inevitably be caught in your own net. It may seem as if the hawk was caught in the net made by the spider, but this is because the spider represents that which the hawk refuses to see. The spider, of course, is not caught in its own net, but it is nevertheless trapped by not being able to leave the net.'

'When the Great Master selected his disciples, he offered the position to more than 12. He came up to many people and said: "Leave your nets and follow me." Many were not willing to leave their nets behind. They missed the opportunity to be students of the Master while he was in embodiment.'

'No human being can fail to be given the opportunity to follow some kind of teacher who can help them escape their nets of perception. The teacher must always approach you by giving you the test of whether you will leave your nets and allow the teacher to challenge your vision.'

'I attempted to do this to you when we first met in the marketplace. You were so caught in the net of a warrior that you were not willing to leave it in order to follow me. I had to allow you to become more and more enveloped in the net, hoping that you would eventually immobilize your outer mind and thus be willing to recognize me when I appeared to you again.'

'The second time you were still very unwilling to leave your net of the wounded and rejected soldier, but you were willing to come to this ashram. This was the opening to the teacher that set you on the path to freedom from the Machine. In the beginning, you were still very reluctant to let me challenge the vision upon which the net was based, but you have fortunately grown to a far greater openness. There are still aspects of your vision that you are not ready to question so I do not challenge them at this time. Rest assured that I will eventually challenge all of the illusions that keep you trapped in the net that is the Machine.'

The Warrior asks: 'Master, what would have happened if I had not followed you the second time?'

'I would have had to leave you behind again. This would have caused you to become even more entangled in the net that can only lead to suffering. Perhaps your suffering would eventually have brought you to the point where you were willing to open your mind to the potential to go beyond suffering.'

12 | The Hawk and the Spider

'Many people have been awakened to the path only through great suffering. This is not what the teacher wants, but the teacher follows an eternal law: "When the student is ready, the teacher appears." The teacher cannot force the student in any way. The teacher can offer the student the path, but it is up to the student's willingness to question his or her vision.'

'Some people can be awakened only through suffering, but suffering is not the only way. It is possible for all people to have a glimpse of a higher vision that allows them to recognize the teacher in whatever form they can grasp at their current level of consciousness. The trick is that you will have such a vision only by being open to seeing beyond your current beliefs, the beliefs that give your ego a sense of security, a sense of being in control. Your progress on the path of self-mastery depends on your willingness to allow the teacher to challenge your perception filters.'

'You can follow a teacher physically without being willing to leave the nets in your mind. You then seek to distort the teacher's message so that it validates your perception filter rather than challenging it. This is a misunderstanding of the teacher and a misuse of the opportunity extended. I am glad that you have not fallen into this trap.'

'My other students will now give you techniques for purifying the third-eye chakra and overcoming the Alpha and Omega perversions of vision. We will then see what animal will appear next.'

13 | THE TIGER AND THE MONKEY

After more time, the Warrior tells the Master about a new dream: 'Master, I have had a very vivid dream that I was a monkey who was innocently playing in the trees, swinging around, eating fruits and playing with my friends. I felt like a perfectly happy child. Then I had to go down to the ground in order to drink from a stream, and while sitting there a tiger suddenly charged from the tall grass and attacked me. I could feel its claws cutting into my leg and when I awoke I was bathed in sweat and my heart was racing. It was the same feeling as when I lost my leg in the desert. I assume the tiger and the monkey represent the next animal pair I will be dealing with?'

The Master replies: 'The tiger and the monkey represent the perversions of the Soul Chakra that is located over the lower abdomen. This is the chakra that is the center for your creative energies.'

'If you look at what society calls "creative people," you will often see that their creative process is filled with tension. This tension is not an inevitable companion of creativity. It is an artificial construct, a combination of people's wounds and the programming of the Machine.'

'In an ideal scenario, creativity would be like children innocently playing in a sandbox. Expressing your creativity is the very foundation for your growth in consciousness. You should be able to freely experiment with your co-creative abilities in order to see what is an expression of your true identity.'

'The Machine has perverted creativity by introducing the idea that your creative efforts have to be evaluated based on a dualistic standard with right or wrong, good or bad. This standard means that instead of freely experimenting, people now go into the analytical mind and seek to compare their creative urges to the standard before they are expressed. This evaluation is completely artificial. You can be creative only by neutralizing the intellect and freely flowing with the creative drive, giving expression to whatever comes from within. You do not know ahead of time what will be expressed. This is creative innocence and when you lose it, there will be an inevitable tension in your creativity.'

'This tension can lead to the two perversions represented by the tiger and the monkey. The monkey represents the rebellion against the standard. Contrary to popular belief, human beings did not descend from the apes. Evolution is not an unconscious process. Apes are designed based on some of the same matrices as the human body, but the human body – especially the brain and nervous system – is a quantum leap beyond apes. That is why only the human body supports the incarnation of self-aware lifestreams.'

'The monkey represents an animal form without the self-awareness that you are an extension of a spiritual being. The monkey may seem playful, but it is not creative play. Some artists have taken their rebellion against the standard of their society to the point where they have suppressed all concepts of following a higher reality. They do whatever they want and refuse to follow any rules. There is a subtle difference here. In order to be creative, it is necessary that you do not follow the rules imposed by the Machine. Yet this does not mean you rebel against a higher order.'

'You are not a separate being but an extension of your spiritual self. Your real identity is not the personality of your soul vehicle but the individuality stored in your I AM Presence. True creativity does not mean expressing the – sometimes animalistic – desires and urges of the body and soul vehicle. Doing this with no inhibition will only create a downward energy spiral that ends up trapping you indefinitely. True creativity means becoming an open door for the individuality of your I AM Presence to be expressed through your soul vehicle.'

'You can express the "personality" of the soul vehicle indefinitely without transcending that sense of self. Instead, you generate a closed system that only imprisons you within more and more narrow boundaries. That is why apes have not evolved beyond being apes and never will evolve into humans. When you express a measure of the creativity of your higher self, you will expand your sense of self and this will gradually help the Conscious You become free from its identification with the soul vehicle.'

'As a truly creative person you are innocently expressing whatever comes to you from the I AM Presence; you are being an open door. You are not evaluating your creative expression based on the worldly standard created by the Machine. You are evaluating your efforts based on how well they express who you truly are. This is not a black-and-white evaluation.'

'Throughout your lifetime, you are meant to grow in self-awareness, which means you become more and more conscious of your true individuality. As this happens, you will naturally become better at expressing your spiritual individuality.

Your life becomes a process where you gradually become more and more creative. In the beginning, you go through an evaluation process where you look at your creative efforts and consider how they reflect your true individuality as you see it. By doing this, you become able to see facets of your spiritual identity and facets of your human identity. This helps you shift your sense of identity away from the human and towards the spiritual, making you more creative.'

'The monkey represents one perversion of this process where you refuse to evaluate your creative efforts and go into a state of mind where anything goes. You begin to think you have a right to do anything you want and that neither man nor God should have anything to say about it. It is not that God wants to restrict your creativity; it is a matter of whether your creative expression frees you from the human or enslaves you in the human. You can know this only by becoming aware of your true identity and beginning the shift away from identifying yourself with the human, the animalistic.'

'The tiger represents the opposite perversion, namely that of not only accepting the standard of the Machine but making yourself an instrument for passing and executing judgments over other people. For example, you will see some people with artistic ambitions who do not dare to go into the perversion of the monkey and throw away all conventions. Instead, they become art critics and now think it is their job to define and enforce a standard for what is "good art." They will – like the tiger – pounce on anyone who does not adhere to the standard they value more than God and often more than human life.'

'You will find these people in every area of society where they set themselves up as those who have a right and an obligation to judge others. They are threatened by creativity, by what cannot be predicted. They want to shut down the creative flow. Some of the worst atrocities in history have been committed by people who thought it was their right to judge others as being not human or as being unwanted, undesirable.'

'In your case, my Son, you have grown up in a society that was almost entirely taken over by this mentality of judging. Most people have accepted that there is a standard for everything. They have not all become judges, although most people do indeed judge those who do not comply with their standard. Most people do not physically execute this judgment, but they have instead submitted to the standard and vowed to live their lives within the framework defined by it.'

'Your father was such a person, and he was an example of what happens to many people. When you suppress your natural creativity, life becomes boring and a struggle, which leads to frustration and anger. Expressing your creativity can only happen when there is a free flow of energy through your four lower bodies. When this flow is blocked, the energies cannot flow freely. This limits your sense of identity and your thoughts. It also prevents the natural flow of your emotions and when the energy of the emotional body is no longer in motion, tension builds. When the tension reaches a critical mass, it will be expressed in these outbursts, which in your father's case took the form of anger. It can also be depression, anxiety attacks, instability or a breakdown.'

'Ideally, a child should grow up in a state of innocence where it is free to experiment without being judged or without experiencing any harsh consequences of its actions. You should be able to play freely without being ambushed by a tiger. The Machine has turned the world into a place where you cannot be innocent for very long. There is always a tiger waiting to jump at you. You quickly learn that in this world, even innocence and the best of intentions can lead to severe consequences. This is not the original condition of earth. It is an artificial construct, created by forces and people who have become blinded by the Machine. The Machine has created a situation where people are constantly struggling against each other.'

'The resulting battle quickly takes away the innocence of even young children. People are not allowed to be children for the time they require but are forced out of this far too early. This often causes them to become like monkeys who rebel, perhaps through drugs or alcohol. Or it forces them to either become judges or to at least submit to the standard imposed by the Machine. In any case, the innocent paradise of what should be a normal childhood is lost and the creative drive is suppressed.'

'Why does the Machine want to suppress people's creative drive? Because the Machine cannot absorb love-based energies but only fear-based energies. The Machine is a structure built from fear-based energies. Anything based on fear becomes a separate system, a closed system, that is cut off from the flow of creative energy that upholds the cosmos.'

'As you know from what science calls the second law of thermodynamics, any closed system will inevitably self-destruct. The Machine is constantly being threatened by the fact that it is outside the creative flow. It cannot itself create or pervert energy. The Machine can survive only by getting human beings to pervert the creative energies so they are turned into fear-based energies. When you express true creativity, you produce only love-based energies. When your creative drive is perverted into the extremes of judgment or rebellion, you produce fear-based energies. That is why many so-called creative people have such tension in their work instead of an innocent flow.'

'The struggle upheld by the Machine is an effect of people shutting down their creativity and the flow of love-based energies from their spiritual selves. In the state of innocence, people can manifest what they need through their co-creative abilities. When innocence is lost, they have to get what they need through physical means.'

'This is symbolized in the story of Adam and Eve who could eat of the fruits in the garden. When they were expelled, they had to work out a living "at the sweat of their brow." The struggle is an effect of the fact that people have to sustain themselves by taking from the finite amount of energy already brought into the physical octave. The original design of the earth is that human beings continue the process of creating the earth by bringing more energy into the physical octave. Thereby, they do not have to fight over a limited amount but can constantly increase the wealth and abundance in this world. Instead of taking energy from others through force, they bring more energy from their higher selves. When you have direct access to the infinite supply of spiritual energy, what is the need for war?'

'My Son, you have made excellent progress. The other students will now show you exercises for invoking the energies of the Seventh Ray, which corresponds to the soul chakra. As you clear it, I look forward to you encountering the last animal pair. When you have attained some clearance of all of your chakras, we can go more deeply into the questions you have about life and your own experience.'

14 | THE COBRA AND THE RAT

After much time has passed, the Warrior tells the Master about another dream: 'Master, I had a dream that I was slowly walking through a forest with dense undergrowth. I was sneaking silently through the bushes when I came across a small clearing and I saw a cobra that was standing up and swerving from side to side with its neck spread out.'

'I looked into the cobra's eyes and I was immediately transfixed, as if I was hypnotized. I had a strong urge to run away but my body would not move. I started moving in synchronization with the cobra, and I felt as if the cobra was sucking the life energy out of me.'

'After what seemed like a very long time, the cobra suddenly lashed forward and bit me. I could feel the venom as a warm liquid spreading through my body. My body became stiff and I felt as if I was suddenly floating out of my body and up above it. When I looked down, I saw that my body was the body of a rat, and it shocked me so much I woke up. I assume this is the final animal pair you mentioned.'

The Master replies: 'Yes, this is the final pair that completes the seven chakras. Many other animals can symbolize what is hiding in the subconscious, and certainly people from other cultures may see different animals for the seven chakras. For you, this is the final pair.'

'I know you have seen a snake or serpent before, but in this case the cobra is the aggressive animal. The coiled up serpent symbolizes the creative energy that is lying latent in the lowest chakra, the base chakra, located at the bottom of the spinal cord at the same height as the sexual organs. This is creative energy, which is not the same as sexual energy. The difference is important.'

'As I have explained before, the Machine has the effect of taking away people's childlike innocence, preventing them from approaching life with the playfulness of the child. This prevents people from taking the creative energy found in the base chakra and raising it in a balanced manner so it activates the higher chakras. Instead, the creative energy is expressed through the base chakra in a horizontal direction whereby it becomes sexual energy. For most people the only way they can express creative energy is through sexual activity or sexual fantasies. As you see so many places in society, sexual energy can be very aggressive, as symbolized by the raised cobra.'

'At the same time, the Machine has managed to induce into most cultures the idea that sex is impure or dirty, something to hide or be embarrassed about.'

'This is symbolized by the rat, which is an animal that is considered dirty or impure and often hides below the ground. As people have for centuries been trying to eradicate or suppress the rat, they have been doing the same to their sexual energies. This has also suppressed their creativity because it has prevented them from openly discussing the topic of sexuality. Sexuality is not inherently sinful, dirty or embarrassing. It can become so when practiced in an unaware manner, which is what has happened to most people. This causes them to feel that sexuality should not be talked about, and this prevents them from making the distinction between creative energies and sexual energies.'

'This in turn makes it almost impossible for them to free their creative energies from being directed horizontally through the base chakra and the sexual organs. They have become reduced to the same state as the rat, which is an animal that only functions in order to eat and propagate. For many people, the circular movement of survival and propagation is what drives their lives. There is no left-over attention or energy for being creative and for pursuing the path that leads to a higher state of consciousness.'

'The cobra symbolizes what has become increasingly common in the modern age. People have now begun to rebel against the suppression of sex. It is indeed necessary that people free themselves from the indiscriminate suppression of sexual energies so common in the past. Unfortunately, this causes many people – even modern society as a whole – to become trapped in the opposite extreme, represented by the cobra.'

'Today, you see sexual images virtually everywhere in movies and advertising. You can read about sex many places. What was before considered dirty is now splashed on the screen of people's consciousness. This is often considered normal. The effect is what you experienced in your dream, namely that people become hypnotized by the cobra that has raised itself up and is swerving from side to side. This is a very aggressive energy.'

'Instead of living like rats focused on eating and propagating, many modern people are hypnotized by the seemingly liberated sexual energies. Instead of being liberated, the people are trapped into constantly fantasizing about sex or feeling they are not having enough sex. It becomes a never-ending quest for filling a desire that is actually insatiable. No matter how much sex people have, something in their base chakra always wants more. This something is, of course, the Machine that sucks out people's energies.'

'The unbalanced desire can be taken to the extreme of having a compulsion for sexual conquest. You now use sex as a way to gain power over people. The extreme outcomes of this is what you see in pornography, prostitution or the sex trade. People, even children, are physically enslaved in order to fill the need for sexual conquest. There are even those who are willing to kill those who will not submit to their demand for sexual conquest.'

'Whenever you see people driven by an insatiable desire, you know they have become slaves of the Machine. A part of the Machine wants to be fed by the energy people misqualify through an unbalanced sex-drive. The unpopular fact is that the so-called sexual liberation has simply enslaved people under another aspect of the Machine.'

'The way to get off the two treadmills represented by the rat and the cobra is to make a distinction between sexual and creative energies. It is perfectly acceptable for people to live in a committed relationship and be sexually active. There is nothing non-spiritual about this. In this age, many people are meant to live active lives in society, which includes having families.'

'You need to avoid that all of your creative energy is swallowed up by sexual desires. The physical body has a programming for propagation and the base chakra can become a black hole of desires that no amount of sexual activity can fill. You can avoid this only by being disciplined, which is not the same as suppressing sexual energies. Through raising your awareness, you will begin to see your creative energies. You will see that liberating your creative energies from being funneled into sexual desires is the way to fulfill your higher, creative desires. This can be to accomplish goals in the material world or it can be to enhance your spiritual growth—or both.'

'When you have become aware that there is something you want more than sexual experiences, you can discipline the energies in the base chakra. Instead of suppressing these energies, you redirect them. Instead of letting them flow horizontally through the base chakra, you set them free to follow their natural tendency to flow upwards. This activates the higher chakras, and this is what gives you the creative power to fulfill material goals or to achieve a raising of your level of consciousness.'

'One of the inescapable consequences of the material world is that it is finite. There is only a certain amount of time, energy and attention available to you in one lifetime. The world is like a store where everything has a price tag. You need to decide how you spend the time, energy and attention afforded to you. You do this by clarifying your desires and making sure that you direct enough energy and attention at fulfilling your highest desires.'

'My Son, you have encountered the base chakra last because it has not been a major issue for you. You have since an early age been able to set aside sexual desires and pursue other goals. You did this while pursuing your goal of becoming a warrior. Even though this was not the highest way to express your creative energies, it still helped you stay free from the treadmills represented by the rat and the cobra.'

'My other students will show you exercises for clearing the base chakra and then we will talk again. As you practice these exercises, I do want you to contemplate whether it is your highest potential to live like a monk for the rest of your life? Is it perhaps part of your life's plan to have a wife and a family? Are there children who would like to have you as their father? I know these questions will shock you, but I want you to contemplate them.'

15 | WHY NATIONS GO TO WAR

One day, as the students are sitting in the assembly hall and have completed their group exercises, the Master looks at the Warrior and says: 'My Son, I see that you have now attained a sufficient clearing of all of your chakras. I do not want you to think this means you have completely cleared your chakras or the subconscious mind. A complete clearance is a long-term, often a lifetime, goal. As long as you are in embodiment, there will be some need for clearing your energy field. What you have achieved now is a sufficient clearance that we can take your path to a new level.'

'When you came here, you had many questions and I have not answered all of them. The reason is that you were not ready to receive my answers. This you need to understand.'

'In the modern age, many people have become blinded by a specific form of thinking. I call it linear, intellectual or analytical thinking. They think the analytical mind is the totality of the mind. They think the analytical mind can comprehend everything. When such people meet a spiritual teacher, they often expect, or even demand, that they should be given a complete explanation of the spiritual side of life. They expect that they will be able to comprehend such an explanation at their present level of consciousness.'

'This makes many people susceptible to the illusions created by the many false teachers in this world. Some of these do not deliberately seek to deceive because they believe in their own illusions. Some know that they are manipulating others. They have deliberately created very elaborate and seemingly sophisticated philosophies in order to ensnare those who make the intellect their God.'

'Many spiritual students think that the more complicated and hard to understand a philosophy is, the more advanced it must be. They think that because they study this difficult philosophy, it proves that they must be advanced students. What neither the false teachers nor their students realize is that these teachers are controlled by the Machine. Their false ideas only serve to uphold and reinforce the grip that the Machine has on all people. As you have seen yourself, the spiritual reality is not that complicated to understand. It requires relatively little understanding but a lot of practical work.'

'What you have experienced over these last months is that you came here with a specific state of consciousness. Your mind was a very unpleasant and chaotic place to be, mainly due to the psychic energies that had accumulated in your chakras and four lower bodies. As you have cleared out some of this energy, you have risen to a distinctly higher state of consciousness in which your mind has more peace and clarity. You are now able to comprehend many things that your mind could not have contained back then.'

'As you cleared out some of the energy, you started experiencing what you had experienced before, namely that what I call the Conscious You stepped outside its identification with the outer mind or self. You have experienced pure, unbound, unlimited, infinite awareness. Without this direct experience, there are many aspects of the spiritual reality that you cannot comprehend.'

'If you think every aspect of the spiritual side of life can be reduced to words or to concepts that the analytical mind can deal with, then you will never fully comprehend spirituality. There are certain aspects that cannot be described in words and cannot be reduced to analysis. They can only be experienced directly through a mystical experience that is beyond words and cannot be reduced to words. This you have now experienced. You can go beyond what the people still trapped in the intellect can do. We will therefore enter a phase where I will allow you to ask any question you have. I will allow you to ask the question any way *you* want, and you will allow me to answer it any way *I* want.'

The chicken or the egg

The Warrior says: 'Master, I see that when I first came, I did not have clarity of mind. Yet I still felt exactly what you said, namely that I should be able to understand the spiritual side of life. I see now how unrealistic that was, but back then you could not have explained it to me. I was indeed frustrated that you did not answer some of my questions, but today I see the wisdom of this. My mind would only have used your answers to create even more confusion.'

'As my first question, I would like to understand why my nation went to war. I see now how it was my personal spiral of anger that caused me to respond when our leader called for warriors. I would like to understand why our nation reasoned that it was necessary and justified to go to war.'

'I know you have said that as a Christian nation, we ignored the call of Christ to turn the other cheek. Our leader, the people in the army and all of my fellow soldiers thought that since the enemy had attacked us unprovoked, it was justified that we responded. The enemy had killed civilians who had never personally done anything to the enemy.'

'We were all fully convinced that if we did nothing, if we turned the other cheek, it would only be seen as weakness and it would encourage the enemy to strike us again and again. We were convinced that our actions were necessary in order to stop future attacks. Master, I would like to hear your perspective on this. What should our nation have done in response to the initial attack?'

The Master says: 'My short answer is that while you went to war because of your personal anger spiral, your nation has a collective spiral. It was this spiral that blinded your nation's leaders to the alternative to going to war. Now, let me give you a longer explanation.'

'My Son, you have heard the old joke about which came first, the chicken or the egg. Now change it a little bit and ask yourself: "Which came first, the action or the reaction?" Clearly, action always comes before reaction.'

'There can be no reaction unless there has been an action some time in the past. This may seem simple, but there is an essential spiritual law hiding here. It says that nothing that has ever happened to you could have happened unless there was a cause that caused it to happen. Remember this principle: no reaction without an action, no effect without a cause.'

'What have I taught you is the key to your personal progress on the spiritual path? What is the key to you raising your level of consciousness?'

The Warrior thinks for a moment, then answers: 'You have taught me to look at my own reaction and to take responsibility for my reaction and my consciousness.'

The Master continues: 'Right. The key consideration here is whether your nation took responsibility or whether it attempted to avoid responsibility. How does this relate to the concept of no effect without a cause?'

Avoiding responsibility

'When you look at history, you see that individual human beings, groups of people and entire nations have always had a tendency to avoid taking responsibility. How do you avoid taking responsibility? You do so by projecting that when something unwanted happens to you, the cause is "out there." You never took an action that caused the event as a reaction. It was other people, faith, life, nature, the world or even God who were responsible for what happened to you.'

'As we have already discussed, when you project that the cause is "out there," you dis-empower yourself. You project that the cause is in a realm where you are not in complete control of what happens. In the case of your nation, it projected that the cause of the attack was found in the realm of the enemy. Since your nation could not control the enemy, it saw no other way to react than to seek to destroy the enemy.'

'A common way to avoid taking responsibility is that you look at an event in isolation. You refuse to consider that a given event can only be a reaction to some previous action. In your personal case, take the event where the bomb explodes and hurts your leg. You could say that you had not personally done anything to the persons who manufactured and planted the bomb. Their actions were a clear aggression against you and it was an unjustified action. You could now become very angry with these people and go on a mission of revenge, seeking to kill them. You could even say that you were doing this to prevent these people from hurting other "innocent" people.'

The Warrior says: 'I actually did feel exactly what you describe. The only reason I did not seek revenge was that my leg prevented me from doing so. Today, I realize that it was not so much my leg but my state of mind that incapacitated me.'

The Master says: 'And that is my point. You did look at the event in isolation and you did project that the cause was in the realm of the enemy. Since you had no physical power to change the enemy, you went into a downward spiral of anger. It gradually incapacitated you psychologically until you were sitting on the street and expressing your anger by yelling profanities at people walking by, people who were not responsible, at least not directly, for your leg being hurt.'

'My Son, my point here is not to make you feel bad about this. My point is to raise a simple question: "Was your reaction the best possible reaction?" When we look at you and your personal future, could there have been a better reaction?'

'As you have experienced now, it was not the best possible reaction. The alternative to building a downward spiral was to build the upward spiral you have built during your time in this retreat. You have done this by acknowledging that even though you had not done anything personally to the people who made the bomb, you had indeed chosen to go to war. You were in their country, you were disrupting their way of life, you could potentially have killed them or their family members.'

'The event of the bomb hurting your leg may not have had a direct, linear cause in your own actions, but it did have an indirect cause. You had chosen to put yourself in a war situation, to put yourself in "harms way," as they say. In the "fog of war" who can predict what might happen?'

'Why did you make that choice? There was a cause in your own consciousness, namely your anger. By looking at the cause in your own consciousness and taking responsibility for it, you were no longer dis-empowered. You stopped projecting that the cause was in the realm of the enemy, a realm over which you had no direct control. You now saw that it was not your only option to seek to physically destroy the enemy. The alternative was to look at your own consciousness and change the cause there, something which you have the potential to take control over, as you are well on your way to doing.'

'The same consideration applies to your nation. Was going to war the best possible reaction, or did it create a downward spiral from which your nation has not yet freed itself? Was there a better alternative, one that could have built an upward spiral?'

'The obvious answer is that your nation could have stepped back and considered what it was in the national consciousness that caused it to be exposed to a violent attack. Has your nation ever in its history committed violent actions outside its own borders? Did it ever send soldiers, agents or corporations to exploit people in other nations? Does your nation have violence in its national consciousness? Does it have a tendency to respond to violence with more violence and feel that this is both necessary and justified? Do your movies and books glorify violence or portray it as the only solution to certain problems?'

'If you claim to be a Christian nation, you should be willing to do what the Great Master told you to do, namely to stop looking at the splinter in the eyes of your brother and to look at the beam in your own eye. This is truly taking responsibility for your situation instead of making your brother "responsible" and dis-empowering yourself. This is taking back your power to control your own destiny instead of allowing it to be controlled by the Machine.'

'Whenever an unwanted event happens in the life of an individual or a nation, the most productive response is to consider what cause you have set in motion in the past that has precipitated this event. With cause I do not only mean physical actions but also your state of consciousness. I have told you many times that the ultimate cause of everything is consciousness. There is always a cause in consciousness that precedes any physical event.'

How consciousness is the ultimate cause

The Warrior asks: 'In one way, I see what you are saying, but I am still confused. I know this is my linear mind talking, but when you say that any event that happens is a reaction from the universe to an action I have taken previously, it makes me wonder what started the sequence? How was it possible to take an initial action when any event is a reaction to a previous action? Who took that first action? I know this may be a silly question?'

'My Son, there are no silly questions, only questions that have not yet been replaced by understanding. First of all, you need to make a distinction between events that you did not directly choose and events that you *did* choose.'

'In your case, you did not directly choose to have a bomb blow off your leg. It is what I called an "unwanted event." An unwanted event never happens "out of the blue," it must have a cause in the past. In your case, the immediate cause was a reaction from the universe to the fact that you were in a war situation. You did directly choose to go to war. You were not forced to do this; you had alternatives.'

'The short answer is that there are three kinds of events that we deal with in the material universe. There are initial actions we take as a result of making a choice. Then there are reactions that are the consequences of some previous initial action. Finally, there are new choices we make as a response to the consequences of our previous actions. This is what for most people have built a downward spiral of action and reaction that obscures the fact that they have power to change their material lives by changing what is in their consciousness.'

'Unfortunately, your culture brings up children without a basic understanding of how the universe works. In the East, you have teachings about karma. It is seen as an action that creates an impulse that will come back to you in the future, possibly in a future lifetime. Your culture denies this because the original teachings of the Great Master on this topic were taken out of the Christian religion for political reasons. Of course, the religion of materialism also denies any preexistence of a soul.'

'Your science has taught you about action and reaction, but most people do not understand this in terms of energy. I do not teach the same concept of karma found in many Eastern religions because I find it too linear and fatalistic. The strictest concept of karma says that everything in your life is predetermined by your actions in a past life.'

'This does indeed raise the question of how you were able to start your karmic spiral. The obvious answer is that you made a choice, but why would your previous choices take away your ability to make choices in the present? I teach that although your past choices have limited the options available to you in the present, you always have the option to change your state of consciousness. Doing this will have profound effects on your physical circumstances, as you yourself have started to prove. It will also have profound effects on what options you are able to see.'

'I teach that when you make a choice and take an initial action, you generate an energy impulse that you send into the universe. Einstein speculated that if you send a spaceship out from the earth and if it continues flying in the same direction, it will one day return to earth from the opposite direction. He said that the space-time continuum forms a closed loop. He was right.'

'What I add to this is that the space-time continuum has four levels or octaves, namely the identity octave, the mental octave, the emotional octave and the physical octave. When you take an action in the physical octave, you generate an energy impulse. This is not what science calls energy, such as electricity or sunlight, but a higher or finer form of energy. It travels into the three other octaves. After some time it will inevitably return to its point of origin, meaning you, and it may then precipitate a physical event.'

Breaking the spirals from the past

'Notice that I said it "may" precipitate a physical event. Whether it does so or not depends on what you have done with your state of consciousness in the time it took the impulse to return to you.'

'This is exactly what the Great Master, and other spiritual teachers, have been trying to tell you by the concept of turning the other cheek. Contrary to official doctrine, the Great Master was fully aware of the principle I am describing here. He was aware that we live many times and that our present lifetime is in fundamental ways limited by choices made in past and forgotten lifetimes. He knew the role of consciousness, and that is why he told you to look at the beam in your own eye.'

'Jesus knew that as a human being in the physical octave, you have a basic choice: Will you continue the spirals you have created in the past or will you break those spirals?'

'When you look at this planet, it is obvious that there is much violence, much use of force. At some time in the past, you made the choice to commit an act of violence against another person. Why did you do this? Because you had patterns of violence in your three higher bodies. In your identity body you had the belief that you are a separate being and that you can use violence against another person without hurting yourself. In your mental body you had sophisticated arguments for justifying the violence. In your emotional body you had spirals of fear, anger or hatred energy that made it seem inevitable to take violent actions.'

'Your physical action was caused by the matrices found in the three higher bodies. It has a non-physical cause. Your initial action created an energy impulse that was sent into the three higher octaves. It was eventually returned to you. As it crossed the border to the physical octave, it precipitated an event where you were exposed to violence. The initial action you took may have happened in a previous lifetime and is now forgotten. What has not changed is that you still have matrices of violence in your three higher bodies.'

'When you are exposed to physical violence, you refuse to acknowledge that this is caused by your own initial action. You project that the cause is "out there" in the person committing the violence against you. This person's actions are unprovoked by anything you have done in the past. You react with anger, and you may take a new action based on violence, seeking revenge or seeking to punish or incapacitate your attacker. This generates another energy impulse that is sent into the universe.

When it comes back, you again react with anger, but this time it is the accumulated anger from all past events. You now send out an even more powerful impulse. When it is returned, the violence you experience is even more severe.'

'You are now trapped in a downward spiral. Your own state of consciousness precipitates violence. Because you refuse to take responsibility for this, you react with violence, which only reinforces the spiral. Pretty soon the energies have become so overwhelming that you are trapped in fear-based reactions. You have lost the ability to turn the other cheek.'

'It is precisely this tendency to react to violent events with more violence that originally created the Machine. Continuing and reinforcing these spirals can only strengthen the Machine and the grip it has on people. The Machine survives through the basic illusion of earth, namely that a physical event that happens to you has no cause in your own state of consciousness. This causes people to react to events based on the attitude that other people caused them. They now go into the reaction of seeking to control or destroy other people.'

'Those other people see your actions as an aggression against them, and they now seek to control *you* through force. Both sides in the conflict feel disempowered because they project that the cause is outside themselves. They see no other way out than to use force to get the other people to change. The Machine has blinded them to the alternative, namely to change your own state of consciousness and thereby change the real cause behind all events that happen to you.'

'How could the planetary downward spiral of conflict ever be broken? Some people have to see the dynamics of the situation and use their ability to choose to respond to violence without violence.'

'The Great Master knew this. He knew that for thousands of years, people had reinforced these energy spirals. Look at how this is still going on in the Middle East and many other parts of the world. That is precisely why he called his true disciples to help break this planetary spiral. There is only one way to do this. It is to stop responding to violence with a violent reaction. You can do this only by turning the other cheek and continuing to turn the other cheek even if you are attacked repeatedly.'

Changing your consciousness changes everything

The Warrior asks: 'Many people would say that the people who attacked our nation must have chosen to take that action, meaning we did not force or cause them to do so.'

The Master replies: 'Yes, the people did choose. Your nation did not force them to choose to attack others, nor did it force them to choose you as the target for their actions. These people were caught in their personal spiral. It was this spiral that caused them to feel a need to take action against others.'

'How did your nation become the target for these people's aggression? Partly because of its physical position and actions, but mainly because of your nation's past spirals. Everything you do is done with energy. It is possible to see the energy spirals that people have created. If you could see this, you would clearly see that nothing can happen to you unless you are vulnerable to such events because of the energy spirals you, or your nation, have created in the past. Unless your nation had an energy spiral that made you vulnerable, you could not have been attacked. Your enemy would have found another target.'

'You always face a simple choice. Will I project that the cause is out there and dis-empower myself? Or will I accept that the cause is in my own consciousness and look there, taking back my power to change my destiny? Yes, the people attacking your nation made a choice, but you became the target because you had also made violent choices in the past. By responding with violence, you will not free yourself from these action-reaction patterns. By looking at your national consciousness and overcoming the tendency to use force, you will indeed produce a peaceful future for your nation.'

The Warrior asks: 'I see what you are saying, but I do not understand how my past actions precipitated a particular event, such as me losing my leg?'

The Master responds: 'The science of quantum physics has discovered the borderline between the physical octave and the three higher octaves. Scientists are aware that beyond the material world is another realm, sometimes called the realm of probability. Nothing in the probability realm has physical, material existence. It exists in a more fluid state where it has the potential to manifest as a physical particle or event. You cannot predict with certainty what will manifest, you can only predict with probability.'

'What scientists have not yet understood is that they have only uncovered a small corner of the process that leads to the manifestation of physical conditions and events. The process also has an aspect that relates to each human being personally.'

'In the past, you chose to perform certain actions. I call them "initial actions" because they initiated an energy impulse that was sent into the three higher octaves. When that energy impulse comes back to you, it starts descending through the three higher octaves. In each octave, the energy impulse will either be weakened or reinforced. The determining factor is the matrices in your three higher bodies.'

'Say you generated an energy impulse through an act of violence. You did this because you had matrices of violence in your three higher bodies. As the impulse returns to you, it first enters your identity body. If you still have matrices of violence here, or if you have reinforced them, the energy impulse will be accelerated by this and move into the mental body. If you had removed some or all of the violent matrices from your identity body, the energy impulse would not be reinforced but would lose some of its power. It would still enter the mental body but with a reduced momentum.'

'The same process is repeated in the mental and emotional bodies. If you still have matrices of violence, or if you have reinforced them, the energy impulse will cross the border to the physical octave. It will then precipitate an event where you are exposed to violence. It may be even more intense violence than the initial action taken by you. If you have transcended all matrices of violence and built a positive energy spiral in your four lower bodies, the returning energy impulse will be completely consumed before it can manifest as a physical event.'

'What you have been doing over these many months by invoking love-based energy is to generate a positive spiral that can consume some of the energy impulses coming back to you from the past. My Son, if you had not done this work but had stayed on the street, you would have been exposed to violence that would have taken you out of embodiment.'

How to turn the other cheek

The Warrior asks: 'I see this now, but I want to understand why it is so hard for us to turn the other cheek. In the army, everyone was convinced that Jesus could not truly have meant to turn the other cheek to all forms of attack. Most people in my country think we have a right to self-defense, even on the national level.'

The Master continues: 'Consider what it would take for a person to follow the command to turn the other cheek. You cannot do this as long as you have matrices of violence in your three higher bodies. These will inevitable overpower your conscious mind. You are not able to choose to refrain from reacting violently when someone strikes you on one cheek. You do not have freedom of choice because the energy spirals in the three higher bodies color your conscious mind. This predisposes you towards either submitting or responding violently.'

'Many people will say that they do not strike back when attacked. Refraining from taking physical action is not the same as turning the other cheek. Many people feel disempowered when attacked or they are afraid they do not have the power to defeat their attacker. Such people do not take violent actions, but they still react with violence, only it is directed against themselves. Forcing yourself to suppress violent actions based on fear is violence against yourself. Only when you are free from fear and feel only love, can you truly turn the other cheek.'

'Only by clearing the energy spirals in the three higher bodies, will you reclaim your freedom of choice. You can then see options that you could not see before. You have the freedom to choose a non-violent reaction, knowing that it will help to set you free from the treadmill of the energy impulses from the past. This is the only way to free yourself from the influence of the Machine. Otherwise, you will remain trapped in the spiral of reacting to violence with violence. This is the Machine's most powerful tool for controlling human beings and milking them for their vital energy.'

'To return to your question of how your nation could have responded to the initial attack, you could have been true to your Christian roots and used the attack as an opportunity to look at the beam in the eye of the national psyche. "How did we precipitate such a violent attack? What kind of violent matrices do we have in the identity, mental and emotional bodies of the collective mind? What could we gain from looking at and transcending these matrices so we do not perpetuate a spiral of violence?"'

'Because your nation was not willing or ready to do this, it reinforced the tendency to respond to violence with violence. It even reasoned that this was justified by the teachings of Christ. Your nation reacted with a more violent force than the force with which it was attacked. This can be seen by the fact that your nation's reaction has killed many more people and destroyed far more property than the initial attack.'

'This has created very powerful energy impulses that are sent into the space-time continuum. They will inevitably be returned to your nation in the future, and they have the potential to precipitate other violent events. There is still a potential for these impulses to be consumed before they cross the line to the physical octave. For that to happen, your nation needs to break the negative spiral and start building a positive spiral by looking at the beam in the national eye.'

'You may feel powerless to do anything about this as an individual, but by purifying your own mind, you have done something to purify the national psyche. If enough individuals do the same, it will have an impact at the national level. After all, the national psyche is a compilation of the individual psyches of the citizens of that nation. The best way to change your nation is to start by changing your own consciousness. The effect you see as physical conditions must follow a change in the cause of consciousness.'

What keeps the spiral of war alive

The Warrior asks: 'What I hear you saying is that the only way to stop war is to stop responding to violence with violence by turning the other cheek again and again. I understand what you are saying, but it is so contrary to the mindset of my nation and especially the mindset of the army. I cannot even begin to see how this mindset could be changed anytime soon.'

The Master replies: 'It cannot be changed anytime soon, but it *can* be changed. Your nation has already entered a course of gradually reducing its propensity for violence. It still has not truly made the shift that will accelerate this spiral and make it irreversible, and that is why the event that sent you to war could happen. If your nation had responded to this event without violence, it would have won an important victory and made the upward spiral irreversible. As it is now, your nation's future still hangs in the balance.'

The Warrior asks: 'Master, what about the people in the army or in the political establishment who say that it is necessary for us to have an army that can defend us against totalitarian nations? They would say that your ideas are unrealistic and they would point to the need for the free world to have an army. They would say that had it not been for the strength and deterrent of the army, the world would have been taken over by Nazism or Communism.'

The Master replies: 'And I would agree with them—up to a point. If you look at the past century in isolation, you do see certain totalitarian forces driven by an aggressive ideology that compelled them to seek world domination. I agree that had the so-called free world (no part of the world is free from the Machine) not had an army, these forces would have attained world domination. Yet how long would they have been able to maintain it?'

'The entire problem in today's world is that the Machine has obscured reality so that people do not see the cause-effect sequences. They do not understand that any aggressive action will generate an energy impulse that is sent into the four octaves. When the impulse comes back to you, this will limit your ability to take further aggressive actions.'

'The challenge of life as it currently unfolds on this planet is that it is indeed possible for an individual to take a violent action against others and seemingly get away with it. It is possible for an aggressive empire to gain control over a large part of the world and get away with this for a time. What people do not see is that this can only be done by generating energy impulses. When these impulses are returned – as they inevitably will be – they will limit the individual or incapacitate the dictatorship. Any force seeking world domination can be successful only for a time. It will inevitably be destroyed by the return of its own aggressive impulses.'

'What the Great Master knew was that if you do turn the other cheek, then you do not make yourself part of the Machine. The absolutely only way to avoid being controlled by the Machine is to refrain from responding to violence with violence.'

'How has the Machine managed to attain control over the world and how does it maintain this control? It does so by putting individuals and nations in a situation where they are exposed to violence or the threat of violence and then making them feel they have to respond to this by using force.'

'When another person makes the choice to use force against you, that person will inevitably generate an energy impulse that is sent into the four octaves. If you follow the advice of the Great Master and turn the other cheek, you will not generate an energy impulse based on fear. You will remain clear of the cause-effect spiral built by the other person. If you respond with violence, you will send a fear-based energy impulse out, and this will draw you into the cause-effect spiral started by the other person.'

The planetary lesson

'My Son, look back at the history of the last 2000-year cycle. Humankind was meant to learn an important lesson during this time. This lesson was taught and demonstrated by the incarnation of the Great Master. His teaching and his example was very clear. It has since been somewhat obscured by the Machine after it took over the religion that claims to represent him. Yet the teaching has still been there for those willing to look beyond official doctrines.'

'What is the lesson? It is that in this cycle, it is necessary for humankind to learn how to break the spiral of violence leading to more violence. This can be done in only one way. When other people take aggressive actions against you, you must refrain from responding with violence. You must turn the other cheek.'

'Surely, in some cases this will cause them to strike you on the other cheek as well. How long should you continue turning the other cheek? Did not the Great Master tell you to forgive seventy times seven? Did he not demonstrate by example that he was willing to die physically rather than compromise his non-violent principles?'

'Did he not say that if you seek to save your – physical – life, you shall lose your life in a spiritual sense? Did he not thereby tell you that if you want to gain immortal spiritual life, you must stand by your principles even if you are killed for doing so?'

'Now consider what would have happened over the past 2,000 years if people had truly grasped and lived the teachings of the Great Master. Humankind would have stopped the downward spirals that cause the Machine to have control over this planet. Instead, an upward planetary spiral would have been built. In that case the world would not have experienced the great conflicts you have seen over the past century. Why is the world seeing these existential conflicts between ideologies, religions and systems of thought? It is because people have not learned the essential lesson. The conflicts created by the Machine have therefore become more pronounced, more extreme. The purpose is to make them so extreme that people finally wake up and say: "This cannot go on. We must find a better way."'

'Why do you think weapons have emerged that are so powerful anyone using them will bring about not only the destruction of their enemy but their own destruction as well? Why do you think it has been necessary for people to experience two world wars? It is because the lesson has not been learned. People have continued to send out energy impulses based on violence. When these impulses are returned by the cosmic mirror, they precipitate even more violent physical events. This will literally continue until a critical mass of people wake up and start breaking the spiral.'

'Your generals and politicians are right in the short term. If your nation had not had a large army over the past century, the world would indeed have been overrun by either this or that totalitarian force. One can therefore say that is was, from a short-term perspective, justified for the so-called free world to resist the growth of totalitarianism.'

'If one looks at this only from a short-term perspective, one will miss the essential lesson. By your country resisting totalitarianism, it has also put itself into the cause-effect spiral initiated by the totalitarian forces controlled by the Machine. This has put your nation even more firmly under the control of the Machine than it was before.'

'Again, the essential way for the Machine to control people is simple. The Machine has taken control over the mind of one person. It now gets that person to take a violent action against another person. If the second person responds in any way short of turning the other cheek, the second person is drawn into the cause-effect spiral. Absolutely any reaction short of turning the other cheek will put you under the control of the Machine. The greater the amount of violent matrices and energies you accumulate in your four lower bodies, the stronger will be the Machine's control over you. This is simply the mechanics of how life currently is on this planet.'

Self-annihilation and self-preservation

'This is also the case on the level of relations between nations or groups of nations. Weapons have now become so powerful that using them would mean suicide. Only this has prevented a third world war. How bizarre is it that humankind has to be brought to the brink of self-annihilation is order to attain at least some willingness to stop the spiral of violence?'

'Your generals and politicians are right that in the short-term it can be necessary to resist large-scale violence. It is also necessary to have a police force to protect people from criminals. Yet one also needs to step back and ask why one lives in a world where violence is common, even why one lives in a world where violence is possible? One needs to ask if there is a better way.'

'The better way was given to humankind by the Great Master 2,000 years ago. If a critical mass of people had internalized his teachings, then humankind would not have had to experience the conflicts you have seen over the past century. Your huge army would not have been necessary. Why does a nation think it needs a huge army? Because it thinks it has a powerful enemy. The peculiar fact is that your enemy thinks it needs its army to defend itself against you.'

'This is the spell that blinds people and keeps them trapped in a spiral of violence. It is a spell that was created by the Machine and it is upheld by the Machine. The Great Master called for his true disciples to wake up and break this spell. If enough people in the modern world heed this call, then the spell can indeed be broken.'

'After the attack that sent you to war, your nation could have looked at the beam in its own eye. There comes a point where one needs to step back. One needs to acknowledge that if one has a powerful enemy, then one needs to ask: "What have we done in the past to precipitate this enemy? What are the spirals of violence in our national consciousness that precipitated this enemy? How long do we want to continue being trapped in this spiral? Is it possible that if we pulled the beam of violence from our own eye, then we would gradually move out of a situation where we are threatened by an enemy? Is it possible we could take control over our national destiny and precipitate a situation where we are no longer threatened by any enemy?"'

'This, of course, is very difficult to do at the national level. It is much easier to do at the individual level where one person at a time wakes up and starts freeing him- or herself from the Machine. As a critical mass of people do this, the nation must inevitably follow.'

16 | HOW THE MACHINE KEEPS PEOPLE TRAPPED

'Master, you have completely opened my eyes. I just had another epiphany by letting your words take me beyond identification with the outer mind. It truly is incredible that our world has been locked in this downward spiral for so long when the teaching was given to us 2,000 years ago. I would still like for you to help me more clearly understand how the Machine manages to keep us trapped in such a downward spiral.'

'My Son, what have I taught you is the underlying reality behind all visible phenomena?'

'Consciousness,' replies the Warrior with no hesitation.

The Master continues: 'You now need to understand the connection between consciousness and energy.'

'The material world is created from energy that falls within a certain spectrum of vibrations. What makes the energies take on the forms, or matrices, you see as physical things and events? It is the matrices held in the three higher octaves.'

'When the earth was created, it was created by a group of spiritual beings who held the very complex matrices for the planet in their minds. They then gradually lowered these matrices through the identity, the mental and the emotional octave. This caused the primordial or spiritual energy to be lowered to the physical spectrum and to take on the forms that you can detect with your senses.'

'The creation of the earth was not finished by the spiritual beings. After it had reached a certain level, new lifestreams started descending to the physical octave and taking on human bodies. They did this in order to learn how to use their creative abilities. They were meant to serve as co-creators and build on to what the spiritual beings had created. By partaking in this act of co-creation, these beings would expand their consciousness, grow in self-awareness and gradually attain the mastery of mind over matter demonstrated by the Great Master.'

'The new lifestreams faced two options. One is that they could co-create from a sense of being connected to the spiritual realm. The other is that they could descend into a lower state of consciousness in which they saw themselves as separate beings. For a long time, no lifestream chose this option.'

'There came a point when some of the new lifestreams did decide to enter the state of separation. As soon as you do this, you experience fear. Out of fear springs the tendency to protect yourself through force or violence.'

'As you take actions through this state of consciousness, you create energy impulses that are sent into the universe. When they return, you do not see that they are consequences of your own choices. You think they are unprovoked events precipitated upon you by whatever condition you fear.'

'You react to this return with more fear and the anger that springs from feeling powerless. This is what creates a downward spiral of fear leading to violence and your reaction to violence leading to more fear and more violence.'

'You now need to understand the relationship between consciousness and energy. Energy cannot take on form by itself. Any form or event you see in the physical octave is the result of some matrix held in the minds of self-aware beings and projected onto the energy.'

'A form in the physical octave does not exist in isolation. It has a parallel in each of the three higher octaves. It is the emotional, mental and identity matrices that can affect the three higher levels of people's minds. Over time, this can create a downward or an upward spiral.'

'When a large number of human beings entered the consciousness of separation, they did so by accepting certain illusory matrices in the three higher levels of their minds. They came to believe in a set of false ideas about the world and themselves. These lies were based on the illusion that the world is separated from its spiritual source and thus people are separate beings.'

Creating energy beings

'Over a long period of time, human beings have held and reinforced these false ideas in their minds. They have allowed much energy to flow through them. This has created large spirals of fear-based energy in all three of the higher octaves of this planet.'

'These energy spirals are created by the minds of individual human beings. When many people reinforce such spirals, they eventually become so intense that they can overpower the minds of individual people. This is how the energy spirals, or the Machine, is able to control people's sense of identity, their thoughts, their feelings and thereby their actions.'

'The energy spirals are formed by energy that moves, much like a tornado or maelstrom. The energy does not have the same level of consciousness as human beings, it does not have self-awareness. Because it is qualified through conscious minds, it does take on a rudimentary form of consciousness. That is why the Machine has an awareness that it exists and that it can continue to exist only by getting energy from human beings. The Machine has enough awareness to have a drive for self-preservation. It knows it can survive only by controlling human beings, getting them to qualify energy with a lower vibration.'

'Because of this mechanism, anything that human beings do creates a matrix in the three higher bodies. This matrix eventually becomes a being with a rudimentary form of consciousness. A family has a collective consciousness as does a nation. Humanity has created a collective consciousness.'

'This collective consciousness is not a homogeneous entity. It has many individual entities that are created out of various thought matrices. One example is a national entity that sees itself in opposition to or in competition with the national entities of certain other nations, even *all* other nations.'

'If you look back at history, you see that many nations had such a national entity or beast. In today's world you see many nations who have modified their national entities so they no longer see themselves as being in a perpetual conflict with other nations. You also see some who have not even started to make this transition.'

'Going back to your question of the mindset of your nation, you see that it has become less fear-based but that there is still some fear. That is why your nation sees the need to maintain a large army. It is also why your nation responded to the initial attack by using the power of those armed forces. The armed forces themselves have also created a collective entity. This entity is by its very nature identified with having an enemy and opposing that enemy. The armed forces of your nation, and the huge industrial complex that makes a profit on building what the army needs, has a survival instinct. How do these beasts secure their own future? Only by keeping your nation locked in a sense of having an external enemy and having to defend itself against any enemy that might arise.'

Capitalism versus Communism

'Not so long ago, the world was locked in a seemingly irreconcilable conflict between two systems, Communism and Capitalism. This conflict eventually faded away, and it did so for two reasons. One is that Communism had created such a powerful downward spiral that the closed system was torn apart by its internal contradictions. The other is that a critical mass of individual people on both sides started to transcend the consciousness that supported both of the giant beasts that were fighting each other in the so-called cold war.'

'Your nation, and many other nations, have started to transcend the mindset of having an enemy. This has happened because many individual people have gone through a similar personal transformation of consciousness as what you have experienced in this retreat. There are not yet enough people who have engaged in this process to decisively put your nation beyond the spirals of war and conflict.'

'This could change, and it could change quickly if enough people became aware of the need to free themselves from the Machine. This is the only realistic hope for ending the very long downward spiral of warfare and conflict seen on this beautiful but troubled planet. Nations go to war because their collective beasts are created based on the illusion that you are a separate being and that you are threatened by other separate beings. Nations go to war because these collective beasts overpower the three higher bodies of a majority of the people in those nations. They can overpower the majority because not enough people have become aware of the spirals and have started freeing themselves from them.'

'This dynamic can be changed by a relatively small number of people. It does not require a majority in order to change the course of a nation or the world. It does take at least 10 percent of the population who whole-heartedly engage in the mystical path, the path of freeing your individual mind from all influence of the Machine.'

The Warrior exclaims: 'Master, I will do anything to be part of that process!'

17 | THE HUMAN DILEMMA REVISITED

One day, the Warrior asks: 'Master, I have meditated on your teachings, and there is one thing that I cannot quite see. You have talked about the human dilemma and how we live in a world that forces us to make choices. Most of us experience this as an unpleasant situation. Something outside ourselves is constantly forcing us to react by exposing us to this or that event. We go from one unwanted event to another. I have started to see how my entire life was a reactionary spiral. I responded to outside events by building my personal energy spiral, and it trapped me in a very small prison where it seemed like I had no way of breaking free. The violence seemed to intensify no matter what I did.'

'I also see how this spiral caused me to react to life with force. While I was at war, I truly felt that any enemy who did not surrender had to be killed. I have now come to see how this entire reaction was wrong. I know you don't talk in terms of right and wrong, but I don't know how else to describe it. I clearly see today that this is not something I would do again.'

'Master, you have talked about taking responsibility, and I have to acknowledge that I killed many people. How do I deal with this? How do I take responsibility for my actions without being overwhelmed by guilt or other fear-based emotions? How do I avoid building another downward spiral that keeps me a slave of the Machine? I have started to see that the Machine is very subtle, and this makes me wonder how we can ever break free from the Machine in a world so completely deceived by the Machine?'

The Master answers: 'My Son, what you are talking about here is a very complex issue. I do not have a magic wand I can wave and resolve this for you. I do not have a snappy statement of wisdom that will make the issue go away. This is one of the most complex issues we must all wrestle with as we walk the path towards freedom. I will take you through a series of steps that might help you.'

The illusion that matter has power over spirit

The Master continues: 'Let us begin by looking at the most subtle illusion perpetrated by the Machine. You have experienced that you are more than the physical body and outer mind, that you are a non-material mind. Until you had the experience of having your leg injured, you had never stepped out of identification with the body and the mind. Most people are still at this stage.'

'When our consciousness sinks below a certain threshold, we lose the conscious awareness that we are non-physical beings and that we have non-physical senses. We now experience life through the physical senses and the outer mind. The matter world seems real, solid and unchangeable. We now become susceptible to the illusion of the Machine, namely that we live in a world of matter and that this world has power over us.'

'Some people have become so blinded by the illusion of separation that they think they are a product of the material world, they are evolved animals. They think their minds are the products of material processes in the brain. Others believe there is a spiritual world beyond the material, but they have never experienced it. They still think the matter world is real and has power over them, leaving them to pray to a remote God to perform miracles for them.'

The deception of the Machine

'The basic deception of the Machine says that material conditions, as they are right now, are the products of processes that are beyond our power to change. We cannot *change* conditions, we can only *react* to them. This makes us feel powerless, and the sense of being powerless leads to fear and anger. This leads to the frustrated attempt to gain control over our destinies by using force. Since it is difficult to use force to change God or the material world, the most obvious option is to use force to seek to change or destroy other people.'

'This builds a negative spiral because the cosmic mirror returns to us the energy impulses we have projected out. As they return, they take the form of physical conditions that are indeed beyond our immediate control. We now feel even more powerless, and the Machine makes us believe that the events that we ourselves created in the past are created by forces beyond our control. Our frustration blinds us even more firmly to the way out, namely to recognize that consciousness is cause and matter is only effect. By looking at the beam in our own eyes and changing our state of consciousness, we can indeed overcome and even change all material conditions. Instead of seeing this, we believe that we can only react to what we ourselves have created. We have become slaves of our own past creation.'

'Why did the Great Master perform what seemed like miracles by healing the sick, raising the dead and giving sight to the blind? He did so in order to demonstrate that the matter world does not have power over our spirits. There is no condition in matter that cannot be changed. Any condition in matter is an outpicturing of the matrices held at the three higher levels. By changing the cause, we *will* change the effect.'

Why you are on earth

'When you begin to see the basic deception of the Machine, you can ask yourself how you can become free from this illusion. This must begin by acknowledging that you are not a material being. You are a non-material being who has descended into the physical body and the outer mind.'

'This leads to the question of why you have done this? What is your purpose for coming into this limited material world? What does the material world have to offer you?'

'The answer is that the material world offers you a unique opportunity for expanding your sense of self and your awareness of your co-creative abilities. The purpose of descending into the matter world is to learn two things. One is how to use your mind to gain control over matter. The other is to avoid letting the material world define you.'

'You are meant to use the matter world to discover more about who you are. You are not meant to let the matter world, and its current conditions, define who you are. Why would you let temporary conditions in the matter world define your ongoing identity in spirit?'

'When you first descend to the material world, you have little awareness of your co-creative abilities. You gain this by experimenting. You are meant to do this as innocently as children playing in a sandbox. The lower energies that make up the material world cannot damage the real you, what I call the Conscious You and the I AM Presence.'

The epic deception

'The Machine wants you to believe that anything that happens in the material world is real. In reality, it is a mirage projected onto the screen of life. This screen can display many different images, as a movie screen can display any movie projected upon it. The current conditions in the world are not unavoidable or unchangeable. They are not the result of an almighty God or an unconscious process of evolution. They are a co-creation between the spiritual beings who created the earth and what human beings have collectively built upon that foundation. Anything human beings have created, human beings can also uncreate. Not instantly, but it can be done.'

'The Machine wants you to believe that current conditions have some epic significance and that it is very important that certain changes are brought about or are prevented. This is contradictory, but every illusion presented by the Machine has an internal contradiction. As an example, some religions say that the world is locked in a struggle between a remote God in the sky and a remote devil in hell. They say it is of epic importance that all people become converted to the only true religion. If they do not, the devil will take over the world and the people will suffer in hell for all eternity. For the sake of the world and for the sake of the individual soul, it is better that those who oppose your religion are killed.'

'The contradiction is that if the world truly is defined by a struggle between God and the devil, then human beings are essentially powerless. What sense does it make that a supposedly almighty God needs you to help him by killing other people? If you truly are powerless, then God does not need your help for you have none to offer. If you are not powerless, then maybe there are better ways of changing the world than by killing other people? Maybe you change the world by using the co-creative abilities given to you by God?'

The birth of the Machine

'When the world was created, the Machine did not exist. The struggle and conflict you see on earth today did not exist in the original design. It is a creation of human beings who have descended into the state of separation. They see themselves as being separated from their source and therefore from each other.'

'This condition is not a disaster and it is not permanent. It is not that something has gone epically wrong with the world. Many individual people simply made a choice to experiment with a lower state of consciousness than the one in which they descended.'

'The challenge is that this consciousness by its nature becomes self-reinforcing. Once you have become deceived by the Machine, everything you experience through your lower state of consciousness will seem to reinforce the impression that you really are a separate being. Only a separate being needs to struggle. The more you struggle, the more chaos you will create, meaning you have to struggle even more.'

'Once you begin to see this, you can consider that the world is not evil. Even the Machine is not evil. The Machine is a vehicle that allows people to have certain experiences that they could not have while seeing themselves connected to the whole. Only a separate being can struggle against and kill other separate beings. The question now becomes whether people have had enough of the struggle or whether they want to experience the struggle in a more extreme form?'

'This question cannot be decided collectively. Once people have stepped into seeing themselves as separate beings, they cannot decide to collectively awaken themselves. Separate beings do have a collective consciousness but it is not conscious. The awakening must happen on an individual level. All you can do is to awaken yourself, which will have a powerful effect on the whole. When enough people do the same, the world will be raised to a higher level where war will become impossible. This has already happened to innumerable planets that are further along in their evolution than earth.'

The world is a sandbox

'The Machine wants you to believe that the material world is real and that the exact shape of current conditions have some epic importance. That is why it is justifiable to kill those who oppose your vision of an ideal world.'

'In reality, the world is like a sandbox. No matter how elaborate are the sand castles you build, it does not change the sand or take away the ability to once again level the sand and make it undifferentiated.'

'The material world is made from undifferentiated energy. It can take on any form, but it cannot be locked in any form. Nothing can take away the potential for erasing all forms or creating new forms. This is what the Great Master demonstrated by changing physical forms through the power of the One Mind. He said that with men, meaning the consciousness of separation, this is impossible, but with God, with the consciousness of oneness, all things are possible.'

'You now see the central mechanics of life. You descend as an unbound spiritual being, but you have a limited awareness of who you are and what you can do. As a new being, you could not create your own world so a world has been created for you. You do not send a child into nothingness but you give it a safe playground.'

'You react to the world in which you descend. By doing so, you send out energy impulses through the four levels of your mind. These impulses cycle through the four levels of the material universe and return to you as physical conditions. As the conditions return, you are aware that they are the product of what you sent out. You can therefore evaluate: "Is this what I want to create, or could I create something more?" If the answer is that you could create something more, you know how to do this. You change your consciousness – the matrices in your four lower bodies – so you project out a different impulse.'

A slave of your own creation

'What has happened on earth is that people have become blinded by the illusion of separation. They have forgotten that the physical conditions they experience now are the results of what they have projected out in the past. They believe in the illusion of the Machine, namely that they have no power to change these conditions but can only react to them.'

'It may seem as if this process has made people the slaves of the Machine. In a sense this is true because the Machine is a collective beast that can easily overpower the minds of unaware individuals. The deeper reality is that you have not become the slave of the Machine but of your own past creation.'

'You have personally created the conditions that return to you. No matter how unchangeable these conditions may seem, you can never lose the potential to uncreate what you have created. No matter what you have created in the past and no matter how much you have reinforced it, you can never lose the potential to break the downward spiral.'

'You can do this in only one way, namely by recognizing that you are a slave of your own creation. You are a slave because you are reacting to what you have created. Because you do not see that you have created it, you naturally cannot change the state of consciousness that created the condition. You unconsciously continue to reinforce that condition, meaning you create new impulses that give you even more of a struggle in the future. You are locked in a spiral of resisting a condition, but everything you do to resist it only reinforces it. You must break the spiral, and you can do so by being willing to look at the beam in your own eye.'

Beyond right and wrong

'My Son, I see from your expression that you are wondering how this abstract explanation relates to your own situation so let us look at that. In this lifetime, you found yourself born into a specific situation. You had an abusive father and your society was forcing you to comply with a certain standard. You resisted this. The reason was that you knew from within that in this lifetime you had the potential to free yourself from the Machine. You resisted submitting to the Machine. Because you did not understand what was happening, your resistance turned into a downward spiral of anger and force. This led you to go to war where you killed many people.'

'You have now awakened. You say that what you did was wrong. I say that the idea that what you did was wrong is a product of the Machine. It is designed to keep you trapped in the reactionary pattern that feeds your energy to the Machine.'

'I say that what you did was an experiment that produced a certain result. You have now realized you do not want any more *of* this, you want more *than* this.'

'The Machine says that what you did in the past was wrong. You need to do something else in order to compensate for what you did in the past. Only when you have done enough to atone for your past sins, will you be free. The reality is that this can never work.'

'What you did that precipitated you going to war was done from the consciousness of separation. Nothing you could possibly do from the state of separation could ever compensate or atone for what was done in the past. Anything you try to do – *anything* – will only create another energy spiral that keeps you trapped by the Machine. You may not be trapped in a spiral of physical violence, but you are still trapped. A gilded cage still keeps the bird from flying free.'

'The only way to truly be free is to fundamentally shift your state of consciousness, your sense of self. You must pull the beam from your own eye instead of seeking to remove the splinters in the eyes of other people. You do this by acknowledging that you are responsible for what you have created.'

The planetary boxing match

'Taking responsibility is a very delicate thing. I see that you have a burning question that blocks your ability to take in my words and the energy carried by them.'

The Warrior says: 'Yes, Master, I understand what you are saying about the sandbox and that everything can be erased. But I still killed other people. How do I deal with that?'

The Master says: 'Did you kill them with evil intent, did you enjoy killing them?'

'No, of course not. I did it because I was blinded by the illusion that it was necessary and justified for a greater cause to kill them.'

The Master continues: 'Even if you had killed them with evil intent, you could still have transcended that consciousness, but for you it is easier to move on. In the army, did you ever have boxing matches?'

'Of course, it was part of our training.'

'When you put on gloves and stepped into the boxing ring, did you feel guilty for giving the other person a bloody nose?'

The Warrior answers: 'I see what you are saying. You mean that because the other person had also put on gloves and stepped into the ring, he knew the risk and I am not really to blame for the fact that he got the bloody nose this time, whereas I might get it the next time?'

The Master says: 'Yes, boxing is just one of the many force-based games people play. All these games spring from the consciousness of separation because only separate beings can struggle against other separate beings. War is a force-based game taken to the ultimate extreme. You may look at your nation and say that the enemy's attack was unprovoked by anything you had done in the immediate past. When you look at the greater perspective, you see that your nation – or at least the people who today embody in your nation – did in the past send out force-based impulses. You also see that these people have not completely overcome the force-based matrices in their three higher bodies.'

'The same is true for the enemy that attacked you. These people also sent out force-based impulses in the past and have not transcended the consciousness behind them. This means both sides have chosen to participate in the war game, as surely as two people choose to step into the boxing ring. You made the choice to go to war and this led to you killing other people. Yet they had made a similar choice.'

Not letting the past define you

'You made your choice because of your personal anger spiral and the collective spiral of your nation. You now face the essential choice of any being who is beginning to awaken from the illusion perpetrated by the Machine.'

'You acknowledge that you are a co-creative being. You are in the material world in order to react to this world based on your present state of consciousness. You make choices and then you react to the consequences of your choices. This is the basic process of how you grow.'

'The challenge for you is to never let the choices you made in the past define you. You are a spiritual being. Your primary task is to never let the material world define you, define your sense of identity, define how you see yourself.'

'The worst thing you can do is to say: "I killed people, that means I am a murderer and I could never be redeemed." This is letting your past choices define you. Instead, you say: "I killed people because I had created an outer self based on the illusion of separation. I now see that I am more than this self. I therefore allow this self to die so that I can be reborn into a higher sense of self."'

'You have two concerns about any choice you make. One is that the choice sprang from a certain – limited – sense of self. The other is that any action creates an energy impulse that is sent into the universe and will inevitably return to you. You will thereby also contribute to the collective spiral that affects other people.'

'Taking responsibility means three things. One is that you realize you are responsible for your use of energy. The energy you have qualified with a fear-based vibration is something you must clean up. You can do this through the spiritual exercises I have taught you.'

'The second aspect of your responsibility is that you transcend the sense of self in which you made the choice. Once you have done this, there is no need to feel guilt for what you did or see it as wrong. In fact, you are now reborn so it is not your current self who made that past choice.'

'The third concern is to test and express your new identity by serving other people, by raising the whole. Thereby, you demonstrate that there is a way to live that is not based on force. You demonstrate that there is an alternative to the struggle and thus you help break the spell that the Machine has cast upon this planet.'

'You do not necessarily have to serve the exact souls you killed or hurt in other ways. It is only important that you give some kind of service to life. This also helps you overcome the identification with the separate self. The key to being free from the Machine is to transcend the separate self that is susceptible to the machinations of the Machine. Do you see this?'

Being spiritually reborn

The Warrior says: 'Master, I once again truly saw what you are saying. I see the need to transcend the old self, but this gives rise to the question of how I can know that I have left behind the consciousness in which I was willing to kill? How can I know that there is still not some subconscious program that could cause me to kill in another situation when I am provoked beyond my limit?'

The Master answers: 'A good question. Let me ask you how you would respond today to the situation where your nation was attacked. Would you again volunteer to go to war?'

'No Master, I would not have volunteered.'

'Why not?'

'Because today I see that killing other people is simply not acceptable to me. It is not an expression of who I am, of how I see myself now.'

'What if your nation had a draft and forced you to enlist in the army?'

The Warrior says with no hesitation: 'I would have refused to go.'

'What if you had been arrested and accused of treason. What if they would have threatened to shoot you unless you had gone to war?'

The Warrior again answers with no hesitation: 'I would still have refused. I would rather have been shot than killing another human being.'

'Why so?'

'Because I am not that kind of a person anymore. I cannot allow my personal anger spiral to be taken out on other people. I no longer will allow the Machine to manipulate me into situations where I feel forced to kill other people. I just wont do it anymore.'

17 | The Human Dilemma Revisited

'My Son, when you reach this point, then you know you have transcended a certain state of consciousness. The Great Master told us that if we seek to preserve our material lives by compromising our spiritual knowing, then we will lose our lives. When we are willing to lose our material lives in order to follow the Master into the consciousness of oneness, then we will attain eternal spiritual life.'

'When you would rather die than compromise your spiritual knowing, then you know you have freed yourself from the hold that the Machine has over you—at least in that area. The prince of this world cometh and has nothing in you. You are reborn and become a new being in Christ.'

'My Son, I see that you are not quite ready to let go of the old self and be reborn. I will ask you to perform some spiritual exercises designed to help you go through this rebirth. Then we will talk again.'

18 | THE PIECES AND THE PUZZLE

The Warrior asks: 'Master, I know you have given me many teachings, but I feel like I have all the pieces for a jigsaw puzzle without having a picture of what the assembled puzzle should look like. I know you have told me that the goal is to put me in control of my life experience. You have also told me that in the material world there is no consequence that cannot be undone. Yet I cannot believe that if I changed my consciousness enough, my lost leg would magically reappear. Is that because I do not have enough faith in your teachings or is there something else I have not seen?'

The Master replies: 'My Son, every teaching must be grasped at several levels. When I said that there is no condition that cannot be changed through a shift in consciousness, this is true, but it is meant to be understood in a larger context.'

'My desire was to help you see that current conditions on earth are the way they are because they have been co-created that way by humankind. Therefore, humankind can change all of the limiting conditions through a change in consciousness. However, the current conditions were created over a very long period of time. It will not take the same amount of time to uncreate conditions, but it will take a substantial period of time, even if all people engaged the spiritual path today.'

What can and cannot be changed

'When it comes to you as an individual, it is true that any consequence you face can be changed. Yet there may be some physical conditions that cannot be changed or that it would take a long time to change. There are some conditions that cannot be changed in your present lifetime.'

'In your case, you have literally lost a part of your body. It was not my intention to make you feel bad or start blaming yourself for not having sufficient faith because you cannot believe your leg could reappear.'

'There are some cases where people can indeed overcome seemingly insurmountable challenges, but there are also conditions that people are not meant to overcome through a physical change. Instead, people are meant to demonstrate that even though they have the physical condition, they can still adopt a positive approach to life and live a spiritual way of life.'

'I suggest that instead of focusing on getting your leg back, you focus on demonstrating how to live a spiritual life with your condition. By doing this, you will begin to shift your sense of self and stop identifying yourself as a cripple. It is truly this shift in identity that I desire to see happen and that I hear you saying that you want to see happen.

18 | *The Pieces and the Puzzle*

What is a mind?

'My Son, think back to your realization that you are a mind. What exactly does this mean? What is a mind?'

'I have never thought about that before,' the Warrior admits.

The Master says: 'Let me make this easier for you by asking you to describe what a mind *does*.'

The Warrior thinks for some time, then says: 'My first impulse was that a mind thinks, but then I realized that it also feels. I then looked deeper and saw that a mind is conscious. I then saw that a mind experiences, a mind is a string of experiences.'

'Once again, you have found the thought I am seeking to make you aware of,' the Master says. 'A mind is an experience "device." Right now, your non-material mind, the Conscious You, is focused here in this physical body. The body is a vehicle for experiencing the material world. The body is constantly being exposed to material circumstances in the form of the situation into which you were born and in which you now live. These circumstances have given you a string of experiences.'

'The experiences have had an impact on how you see yourself. Most people identify themselves as the physical body, as a material being that is a product of the circumstances to which they have been exposed and the experiences they have had as they reacted to the external circumstances. What you have been going through in this retreat is the process of breaking the bond between the physical body and your outer circumstances on one side and your sense of identity on the other side. You have started to realize, and even experience, that you are more than the experiences you have had in the material world. You have started to see that although the experiences have affected you, they cannot define you completely. When I say that any consequence can be changed, I mean that your mind can change the impact that any experience has had on your sense of identity'

Two levels of experiences

'I have talked about the fact that you have a higher part of your mind, which I call the I AM Presence. The Conscious You is an extension of the I AM Presence sent into this world. The purpose is that your Presence can express its creative powers in this world and then experience this world. By doing this, your Presence will expand its sense of self.'

'I know this is abstract, but as you perform the spiritual exercises and clear your four lower bodies, you will begin to have a clearer sense that you have a higher self. Has that been your experience?'

The Warrior answers: 'Yes, I have indeed had many experiences of what you call pure awareness where I do not experience the world through the filter of my four lower bodies. I have also had experiences of being connected to something greater than my individual self. I have had a sense of receiving unconditional love from this greater part of my being and even getting a perspective on my situation.'

The Master continues: 'These experiences are a natural consequence of purifying yourself from the chaotic energies and false beliefs in your four lower bodies. Many people who are open to the spiritual side of life are open because in past lives they achieved some direct experience of being connected to something greater. For many people, what drives their spiritual quest is indeed a deep inner longing for connection or oneness with something. They often are not aware of what it is, but it is truly their own higher beings. We have a deep inner sense that there is something beyond our limited selves, and we long to once again experience the wholeness that can come only from our higher selves.'

'We now need to add the concept that although your mind is an experience machine, it can have two levels of experiences. Every situation you have ever encountered on earth has been experienced by your I AM Presence. What can be difficult to grasp is that your I AM Presence does not experience a situation the same way you normally do with your conscious mind.'

'Your I AM Presence is located in the spiritual realm. It experiences the material world through the Conscious You. We can say that the Conscious You is like a periscope through which the I AM Presence can see into this world.'

'This is easy enough to grasp. The difficult part is that although the I AM Presence looks at the world through the Conscious You, it does not see the world the way the Conscious You does. The reason is that the Conscious You normally experiences the world through the filter of your four lower bodies. The I AM Presence is completely unaffected by this filter and sees the world without any coloring.'

'Your true, spiritual identity is stored in your I AM Presence. What people normally see as their identity or personality is the contents of their four lower bodies. This is not your true identity. It is a temporary identity that you have taken on as you reacted to this world. Your I AM Presence experiences every situation through your spiritual identity and it has an entirely life-supporting experience. Your Presence sees and uses every situation as an opportunity to grow. In some cases, the Presence uses a situation to define what it is not, but this still expands your sense of self. We can say that in every situation your I AM Presence has one experience and the Conscious

You has another experience. The goal of the spiritual path is to remove this division so that your Conscious You experiences a situation the same way as your I AM Presence. Instead of two experiences, you have one.'

The lost paradise

'The Conscious You first descended into the material world many lifetimes ago. You cannot rise beyond a certain level of the spiritual path without accepting reincarnation. Growing spiritually means dealing with the complexity in your subconscious mind. As you go to deeper layers, you will encounter a complexity that could not have come about in one lifetime. I know you have seen this.'

The Warrior nods, and the Master continues: 'When you first descended into this world, you did have four lower bodies. These bodies were like empty containers that had very little content. They did have some content related to using the physical body, but they did not have the complexity or the personality you find now. They served as the connecting link between the Conscious You and the physical body.'

'The Conscious You was the connecting link between the I AM Presence and the body. It was the individuality in the Presence that determined what you did in this world. Your life experience was not the same as that of the Presence. You experienced life like an innocent but inexperienced child. You felt connected to the Presence and you knew that nothing in this world could define you or even limit you.'

'This state of mind is the basis for all of the many myths about a lost paradise. The story of the Garden of Eden can be seen as a myth about The Conscious You (Eve) and the I AM Presence (Adam) being in a wonderful place accompanied by their spiritual teacher (God). The concept of a lost paradise is the loss of your conscious awareness of your higher self and spiritual teacher.'

'How did you lose this edenic state of mind? It started because the Conscious You gradually began to put contents in your four lower bodies. This was a natural part of your growth process. You started defining certain ways of reacting to the many repetitive situations life presents to you.'

'As this process continued, the contents in your four lower bodies became more complex. They eventually took on a life of their own and formed what I call the outer self or ego. There was nothing inherently wrong with you building this self, but as it became more complex, you faced the spiritual initiation represented by the story of the serpent tempting Eve to eat of the forbidden fruit.'

'The forbidden fruit is a symbol for the possibility that your Conscious You can step into the outer self and thereby come to identify yourself with and as this separate self. By doing this, you will inevitably lose your conscious awareness of your I AM Presence. You cannot at the same time see yourself as being connected to the Presence and as a separate being. You cannot be in two states of consciousness at the same time. Once you stepped into the separate self, the paradise of being connected to something greater was lost.'

'Again, there is nothing inherently wrong with the Conscious You deciding that it wants to experience the material world through the filter of the separate self. It is an experience you are allowed to have. For many it is necessary to have this experience as part of their growth towards a greater sense of self. The trick is that once you step into the separate self, you will experience yourself as being disconnected from the I AM Presence. A separate being is separate from the I AM presence but also from all other separate beings in its environment. It is also separate from its environment and from God, whom it now experiences as a remote being in the sky rather than as an inner Presence. This separation leads to conflict, meaning the life of a separate being is one continuous struggle.'

The impossible quest

'The separate self is engaged in an impossible quest. It is attempting to reclaim the lost paradise, which the Conscious You cannot completely forget. The only real way to do this is to reestablish your conscious connection to the I AM Presence. The separate self can never do this so it attempts to establish a "paradise" here on earth by creating a state in which it has everything it desires and can never lose it. This is impossible because life, nature and other people are constantly interfering with the separate self's quest. This is what makes your life a struggle and you can never overcome this through the separate self.'

'The question now becomes how long you want to experience the world through the separate self before you feel you have had enough of the struggle and want something more. When a person begins to become conscious of its longing for something higher than what the material world has to offer, then it is a law that the person must be presented with a teacher or teaching that can help the person rise to a higher level of consciousness. When the student is ready, the teacher must appear.'

'The tricky part is that the teacher comes to help the student become free from at least some aspect of the outer self. The student will always experience the teacher through the filter of that outer self. This makes it very difficult for the student to grasp the teacher's message.'

'You will remember that the serpent in the Garden of Eden said to Eve that if she ate the fruit, she would become "as a god, knowing good and evil." This symbolizes the state of mind of the separate self. It believes it is a god who can define what is good and evil, true and false, real and unreal. As long as the student looks at the teacher through this filter, it will often reject what the teacher is saying. I assume you can see this?'

The Warrior says with a smile: 'Yes, as I was taking in your words, I saw how I used to argue in my mind against everything you told me. I can only wonder how you had the patience to put up with my constant rebellion against your attempts to do what my inner being wanted.'

'My Son, you do not think that I was always a teacher, do you? I too was once a student, and I also argued against my teacher. Because I have gone through the same process as you, how could I not show you the same patience that my teacher showed me?'

Being ready for a teacher

The Master continues: 'As our next step, let us look at a situation you encounter here on earth. It can be any situation so let us keep it non-specific. As you encounter the situation, you experience it at two levels. Your I AM Presence experiences the situation through your spiritual identity and has a life-supporting experience that helps you grow at that level.'

'Your Conscious You experiences the situation through the filter of the outer personality. It reacts to the situation based on the personality of your outer self. This personality is a set of reactionary patterns, very similar to the code in a computer that causes it to always react the same way to certain stimuli. Your reaction to the situation affirms and reinforces the outer self. As you have experienced yourself, once you have a pattern of reacting with anger, almost any situation will add to the maelstrom of anger energy in your emotional body. It will affirm the mental and identity beliefs that make you feel justified in reacting with anger.'

'Your separate self literally becomes a self-fulfilling prophecy. Here is how this works. The issue we face is that you are in this world in order to expand your sense of self. You are allowed to create a separate self, but if you become stuck in it indefinitely, it will work against the expansion of your sense of self. The issue becomes how to make sure that you cannot remain stuck in this self forever.'

'This is accomplished through the basic design of the world, namely that everything you do is done with energy. We can say that the universe forms a mirror, but a mirror that reinforces what it reflects back. If you send out an energy impulse of anger, you will receive back an even stronger impulse. This means your personal anger spiral will gradually be reinforced until it finally becomes so intense that it swallows up your life. The purpose is simple.'

'As I said, once you step into the separate self, you cannot easily hear what a teacher tells you. You are unreachable for those beings who are still in oneness. If your state of separation could remain constant, as your separate self desires, you might never get out of it. Because your struggle intensifies, it will eventually become so intense that you long for something more, you long for peace, you long for the lost paradise. It is then that you become open to the teacher.'

'When you are open, a teacher must appear. That is why the Great Teacher appeared to humankind 2,000 years ago and why other teachers have appeared before and after. As we have discussed, most people did not use the teacher's message and example in order to free themselves from the separate self.

They took the teacher's message and interpreted it through the separate self, thereby creating a religion that only intensified the struggle by justifying wars, crusades, inquisitions and witch hunts.'

'What blocks your acceptance of the teacher's message is that the separate self is entirely focused on material conditions, including consequences. In your case, it was losing your leg that shocked you out of identification with your separate self. Yet the admittedly harsh physical consequence almost made it impossible for you to accept me as a teacher.'

Undoing consequences

'We have now returned to the question of how consequences can be undone. What is a consequence? Your outer self says it is the actual physical condition. Your Conscious You has the ability to step outside this perception and realize a profound truth.'

'A mind is an experience device. In reality, a consequence is not the physical condition but your *experience* of the condition.'

'It is not the physical condition that affects your life experience. It is how your outer self reacts to the physical condition.'

'You are constantly conscious of yourself and of life. Your life experience is this ongoing state of awareness. You have lived many lifetimes before this one, and in those lifetimes you experienced many physical conditions that are now forgotten. Those physical conditions are now gone, they are non-existent, they have been erased. Yet your reactions to those conditions still reside in your four lower bodies. They form a filter, and as long as the Conscious You is looking at life through that filter, it will form your life experience.'

'How do you truly undo a consequence? You do not do so by changing the physical condition. You do so by changing the patterns in your four lower bodies that form your perception filter and therefore affect your life experience. Your outer self is like a pair of colored glasses. As long as you are looking through the glasses, they color your experience. As soon as you take off the glasses, the effect is undone.'

'Undoing a consequence is a two-fold process. One aspect is to free the Conscious You from its identification with the outer self. The other is to dissolve the components of the outer self, meaning the fear-based energy spirals and the false beliefs about yourself and the world.'

'Once you have accomplished this, the consequence will no longer affect your life experience, even if the physical condition has not changed. Therefore, the consequence has been undone where it truly matters, namely in your experience—which is all that you are.'

'In your case, your I AM Presence is focused on your Divine plan for this lifetime. An important part of this plan is that you can serve to help other people overcome their identification with the separate self. For your I AM Presence, your physical body losing a leg is no hindrance for your Divine plan. It can be used constructively because it is simply one more condition that you can overcome and therefore serve as an example for others.'

'Your outer self is completely obsessed with you losing your leg. When we met, your outer self had used this consequence to block your Divine plan by getting you in an agitated state of mind. The event that was meant to awaken you was being used to put you in an even deeper state of sleep.'

'My Son, tell me about the experience you are having by listening to my words.'

18 | The Pieces and the Puzzle

The Warrior looks at the Master with a big smile and says: 'I was once again taken out of my body and outer self by your words. It was like I was riding the wave of energy that your words formed, and I experienced the reality of what you are saying. I know my intellect can understand your words and they make sense. But I literally *experienced* that I am a mind and that I have an alternative to looking at life through the outer self. I experienced the calmness of how my I AM Presence looks at life. It is almost as if my Conscious You became completely neutral and was free from the emotional patterns of the outer self. It was free from judging every situation based on this standard of right and wrong, good or bad. Master, is this how you experience life?'

The Master replies: 'Yes, after walking my own path for many years, I did arrive at the point of returning to the lost paradise in which my Conscious You is not pulled into any reactionary patterns. I experience life with the childlike mind that the Great Master said is the only state of mind that gives us access to the kingdom, the kingdom he said is within us. The path truly is about reclaiming our lost innocence, which has never truly been lost.'

'The separate self can maintain its existence only as long as we believe that what we experience through it is real. Yet it is only an experience. What you see through your sunglasses does not change the sun; it only changes your perception of the sun. Once you undo the energy spirals and the beliefs that make up your separate self, the experience you had through that separate self no longer exists. Therefore, it no longer affects your life experience. You are free. Eventually, you will be free to experience life in the material world the way your I AM Presence experiences life. I hope you will one day join me in paradise.'

19 | THE WARRIOR SURRENDERS THE WARRIOR

Time passes. One day the Warrior tells the Master: 'I have contemplated your latest teachings about a mind being an experience device and how to take command over my life experience. In meditating upon this, I had an experience similar to when I was seeing the different animals, only this time it was not an animal form. In fact, it was as if I sensed a being that had no form but that was either invisible or like a chameleon that could change colors to blend in with the background.'

'I eventually came to see this more like a self, and it was very subtle and persuasive in attempting to get me to reject your teachings. It tried all kinds of arguments in order to convince me that it is not only my life experience that matters. It almost seemed desperate to get me to hold on to the idea that conditions in this world are real and that they really do matter.'

'You have taught me to always look deeper so I used the spiritual exercises to work on the energy associated with this self and I also tried to look at it from different perspectives. I can see that it really has to do with the idea that I have to win because if I don't win, I am a looser. I feel this must be what you called the warrior self because it really wants to win, and to this self it seems like there are only two possibilities. Either you win or you are no good at all. Losers have no value to this self so it becomes almost a matter of life or death that you win at all costs. Master, can you give me some insights on this?'

The Master replies: 'I have been waiting for you to begin to see this. I wanted you to see this first on your own because it was important that I did not lead you in any way. It had to come from inside yourself. What you have now uncovered is, as you have sensed yourself, the core of your warrior identity or self.'

'This is not only a self that applies to a warrior. We might say that the warrior self is just one persona that a deeper self can take on. This self is the deepest challenge for all spiritual students. It is the separate self that ties you to the material world.'

The inescapable conflict

'I have told you that you started out as a pure and innocent being, meaning that while you had four lower bodies, you had not experimented with the consciousness of separation and you had not created a separate self. At some point in your past, you did experiment with separation. You created a separate self and you came to identify yourself with that separate self. This applies to all people on this planet. We simply would not have embodied on a planet with as low of a consciousness as earth, if we had not created a separate self.'

'As I have said before, there is nothing inherently wrong with doing this, as free will gives us the right to have this

19 | The Warrior Surrenders the Warrior

experience. The problem is that the experience becomes self-reinforcing. When you identify yourself with and as your separate self, your perception of the world is limited to the physical senses and the outer mind. The senses and the outer mind are created in order to function in the material world. To them, the material world seems completely real. The separate self is also created in order to deal with the material world. To this self, the world seems not only real, it also seems very important. The separate self is convinced that the world has epic importance and that it is conditions in this world that will determine your future survival, even your eternal salvation.'

'To the separate self it is necessary to bring about certain conditions in this world in order to secure your survival or the survival of civilization. The separate self is also convinced that your eternal salvation depends on fulfilling conditions in this world, rather than giving up the conditions that keep you tied to this world.'

'The separate self is born out of the consciousness of duality, meaning there will always be two opposites. One example is Communism and Capitalism while another is God and the devil. To the separate self, bringing about the right conditions in this world inevitably involves a conflict. There is an adversary that must be defeated in order for you, your civilization, your thought system or even God to win.'

'This explains the many wars you have seen on this planet. Human beings know instinctively that it is wrong to kill other human beings. Overriding this requires justification, namely that there is some cause that is so important that it justifies killing. This has perverted many religions so that it seems to people that the same God who gave the command "Thou shalt not kill" now justifies and rewards killing those who oppose your religion.'

'This epic mindset has caused numerous people to do things that they know within are not truly the highest way. Once you have done something based on the epic mindset, it becomes very difficult to admit this. If you cannot admit that something you did in the past is not what you want to do in the future, then you cannot free yourself from the past. You become sucked into a never-ending spiral of seeking to justify what you did and thereby justify the separate self. Many people have their entire lives swallowed up by such a spiral of justification. Often, it is not their personal actions they seek to justify, but those of their nation, thought system, political ideology or religion.'

A tricky process

'My Son, having uncovered this self is truly a milestone on the spiritual path. Of course, you now need to free yourself from it.'

'It is a good observation that this self has no form or is like a chameleon. Truly, the separate self has no form. It seeks to make you attached to form, and that is why it can take on various forms in order to blend in with the culture in which you live. In a religious culture it will take on the images used in that religion. In a communist country it took on the shapes defined by ideology. In many modern democracies it takes on the shapes defined by the materialistic mindset. It is a great challenge to overcome this self while being in a physical body that is naturally so dependent upon the material world.'

'Different people will have slightly different challenges when they start seeing their separate selves. In your case, your separate self has taken the form of the warrior self. You have now started to adopt a spiritual mindset and you have a goal of

19 | The Warrior Surrenders the Warrior

raising your consciousness, thereby freeing yourself from the Machine. As you begin to see that you have a warrior self, you are still not free from this self. You tend to look at the warrior self through the perception filter of the warrior self. Have you noticed this?'

The Warrior replies: 'I see what you are saying. I did begin to feel that the warrior self is an enemy of my spiritual growth and that I need to find a way to defeat it.'

'Very good,' the Master says, 'can you then see what is the problem with this feeling?'

The Warrior thinks carefully for a time, then shrugs his shoulders and says: 'Master, I just can't see this.'

'My Son, close your eyes and focus your attention in your heart. Now ask yourself a question: "Given what I know about action and reaction, can I ever defeat my warrior self by fighting it?"'

The Warrior almost jumps in his seat and exclaims excitedly: 'Master, *now* I see it! I really saw what you are saying. The Warrior self is based on defining an enemy and then fighting it. If I define my warrior self as an enemy and start fighting it, I can never be free from it. The more I fight the warrior self, the more trapped I become. Boy, what an incredibly tricky process this is. I mean, how did we ever get ourselves into this situation where things are so damn subtle? How will we ever get out of this without having teachers like you?'

The Master replies: 'Once we have stepped into separation, we will never get out unless we make contact with a teacher who is outside separation and can offer us an alternative experience. This is proven by the fact that after thousands of years people are still warring with each other with no end in sight. The law says that when the student is ready, the teacher must appear and many teachers have appeared in this world. A teacher can help you by giving you teachings and tools, as I have done. A teacher helps you most by demonstrating to you that it is possible to live your life in a way that is not controlled by the separate self. When you first came here, you were completely identified with your separate self. You experienced that I was *not* identified with your separate self, and this gave you a perspective that was more valuable to you than you might realize. It showed you that there is something outside the closed system, the self-reinforcing spiral, of the separate self.'

Why you cannot defeat the separate self

'I now want you to take my teaching on energy and apply it to why you cannot defeat your warrior self with force. The very moment you define an enemy, you also go into a mindset of thinking you have to use force in order to either protect yourself from or defeat that enemy. Fear is based on the idea that something can threaten you through force. Naturally, you then think the only way to protect yourself is through force.'

'I am not here talking only about physical force but also psychic force. You may fear an enemy and although you do not take physical action, you are sending impulses of psychic energy into the four octaves of the universe. I have told you the space-time continuum acts like a mirror and returns to you what you send out, only multiplied.'

'Say you discover that you have a warrior self that blocks your spiritual progress. You decide that this self is your enemy and you start directing your psychic energy at defeating the warrior self. You thereby generate a force-based impulse that has a certain intensity or strength. Let us define a scale and say that your impulse has the strength of 2 on the scale. The impulse now cycles through the four octaves and returns to you with the strength of 3 on the scale.'

19 | The Warrior Surrenders the Warrior

'You experience this return as an opposition from your warrior self. It could also be that you see it as opposition from an external enemy, the principle is the same. You now feel threatened by this returning force and in order to free yourself from its influence, you generate a new psychic impulse with the strength of 4. This gives you a temporary relief, but you have now sent an impulse into the continuum with the strength of 4. This will inevitably be returned to you as an impulse with the strength of 6. You must now generate a new impulse with the strength of 7 in order to feel some relief. Of course, it will be returned with the strength of 10.'

'This can go on until you have generated an impulse with the maximum strength that you are capable of, given the state of your four lower bodies. You have used all of your psychic strength to generate this last impulse. Obviously, it will be returned by the universe multiplied, meaning you do not have the strength to overcome it.'

'Before you reach this breaking point, you feel like you are always behind, like you have to run faster and faster. This is what in the modern age is called stress. Look at how many people feel like no matter what they do, it is not enough or good enough. The cause is that people are using force to fight what they see as a threat from outside themselves. In reality, they are fighting the psychic impulses that they themselves have generated in the past.'

'This can go on for a long time, for some people an entire lifetime. In today's world, increasing numbers of people are reaching the breaking point where they do not have the strength to defeat the return current. This causes them to experience a breakdown, which can be a physical disease. Yet increasing numbers of people experience a psychological disease, such as depression, angst or a more severe breakdown. My Son, can you see that given the nature of the cosmic mirror, you can never get out of the force-based mindset by using force. You simply cannot defeat the universe?'

'Yes, Master, I saw this very clearly as you were speaking. So how do I defeat the warrior self, or rather free myself from its influence?'

The modus operandi of the separate self

'You do so by doing the one thing that the warrior self does not want you to do. What was the slogan you used in the war?'

'Do you mean "Never surrender?"'

'Yes, is not the nature of the warrior self that you must keep fighting? You must never surrender because that makes you a looser and being a looser is the worst thing the warrior self can imagine. Tell me about your reaction to my words.'

The Warrior replies: 'Master, I suddenly felt like this gigantic wave of energy washing over me. It was my warrior self, and it still had no form but it was so tangible that I could feel it with all of my senses. It was saying that what you are saying is the worst nonsense it has ever heard and that it is the lies of the devil because the last thing I must ever do is to surrender.'

'I am literally feeling like I am sitting outside myself watching my warrior self rage like a boiling ocean. It is almost amusing to me even though the energy is very intense right now.'

The Master says: 'It is very good that you feel like you are outside the warrior self. You have heard the saying that one can win a battle and lose the war. This is what the warrior self wants you to do. It wants you to focus on winning some battle in this world by making you attached to a particular result or outcome. By doing this, you have no psychic attention or energy left over for freeing yourself from the separate self. You are losing the war even though you think you are helping to

19 | The Warrior Surrenders the Warrior

win the war defined by the epic mindset. You are loosing the "war" for your own freedom from the Machine.'

'My Son, there is only one way out of your identification with the separate self, whether it takes the shape of a warrior self or something else. You must identify its basic belief, its modus operandi, and then do the opposite of what it tells you to do. The separate self is based on wanting to control something in this world, wanting to bring about a specific outcome in order to produce a change of epic importance. Once you identify this, you can also see how to break the spell by not doing what your separate self wants you to do.'

'By doing this, you put the separate self in a dilemma. Most people have no idea that they have a separate self. This means their separate selves are in an ideal position where they can control people without exposing themselves. The separate self can survive only by staying hidden, meaning the way to overcome it is to force it out in the open where you can see it and see that it is not the real you.'

'You do this by coming to see its basic mindset and then challenging this. A good teacher can help you do this, but ultimately you must see it from within. When you identify the modus operandi of your separate self and begin to question it, the separate self must attempt to get you to stop doing what you are doing. It cannot do this without exposing itself to those who pay close attention. This is the simple, but effective, way to free yourself from the separate self in any form.

'Your warrior self is telling you to keep fighting and to never surrender. You have now seen that the fighting is futile because you can never defeat the return current from the cosmic mirror. You will only have your life swallowed up by a meaningless and inconsequential struggle. The outcome that the warrior self has defined, can never be achieved. Even if it *could* be achieved, it is still not God's cause, or whatever epic goal has been defined. In reality, it serves only one cause, namely to keep you trapped in the Machine and to keep the Machine alive.'

'The Great Master told us to lose our lives in order to follow him. The deeper meaning is that we give up, surrender, the "life" or goal defined by our separate selves. We see that leaving our nets is necessary for us in order to follow Christ into a higher state of consciousness. We see that surrendering the attachments of the separate self is the key to winning the ultimate victory of being free from the Machine. Surrender is the ultimate key to victory.'

'When you see this, you can surrender the entire mindset. You can decide that instead of seeking to win the fight, you will simply walk away from the battlefield. You will not be attached to producing a certain outcome, to winning the final or decisive victory that is always around the corner. You will not be attached to other people or your separate self calling you a looser, a pacifist or a narcissist. You will simply walk away from the fight.'

'My Son, I am not saying you *can* do this right now. I am not saying you *cannot* do this right now. I am saying that as you contemplate these concepts and use the spiritual tools to transform the energies that tie you to the struggle, you will one day come to a moment when something breaks in you. Your tie to the struggle has broken. You simply walk away from the battlefield without looking back.'

Using a spiritual teaching to struggle

'I have seen so many spiritual students find a spiritual teaching and have their eyes opened to the need to change the world. I have seen them reason that the key to changing the world is to convert everyone else to their system or guru. They have then engaged in a process where they think they are working for a spiritual cause. In reality, they are using a spiritual teaching as a justification for engaging the force-based struggle.'

'This is subtle. I am not saying that spiritual people should withdraw from the world and avoid taking active part in society. I am only saying that they might need to withdraw for a while until they have freed themselves from the force-based mindset.'

'Regardless of your good intentions – what the road to hell is paved with – you will not help change the world by seeking to do so from the force-based mindset. You will change the world only by freeing yourself from the force-based mindset and then going out in society without this mindset. You can then be an example for others that there is an alternative to the force-based mindset. If enough people do this, then we will actually make progress towards bringing about a more peaceful world.'

20 | THE WARRIOR LEAVES AND RETURNS

One day the Master says: 'My Son, we have talked about your Divine plan and your potential to help others. Tell me what you see as the next step that will empower you to start giving service to life.'

The Warrior sounds hesitant: 'I am not sure I see what you are saying, can you help me?'

The Master replies: 'My Son, we both appreciate honesty. Do not tell me that you cannot see what is the next logical step in your life. Tell me honestly why your outer mind is not willing to acknowledge what you clearly see at inner levels of your being.'

The Warrior looks flustered and answers: 'Well, there is a part of my mind that does not want to see the obvious because it means I would have to leave your ashram. I know I will miss you and I am scared about going back out into the world. I feel like I want to spend more time here with you until I am ready.'

When will you be ready?

'My Son, if you wait until you are ready before you do something, then you will never get anything done in life. Why not? Because life is about overcoming a limited sense of self. Your limited self will never be ready for a certain task. You start the task before you are ready so that your only way to complete the task is to transcend the separate self. You can complete any task by being willing to transcend the separate self that says the task is impossible.'

'Being ready is a delicate balance. You do need to make certain progress before you are ready to take the next step on your path. In your case, you needed to spend time here, contemplating my teachings and invoking spiritual light to purify your energy field.'

'There always comes a point where you have done enough inner work that you are ready, only your outer mind will not recognize this. Your ego will come up with all kinds of reasons why you should wait until this or that important thing has happened. The reality is that once you have done the inner work, you will not be ready until you decide that you are ready—*now*. So tell me what you know is the next step.'

The Warrior responds: 'You are right, Master. I actually learned about making honest decisions by being in battle. You could not hesitate or you would die, you had to be decisive. I know from within that my next logical step is to go back and take advantage of the government's offer to give me an artificial leg. With training, it is almost certain that I will be able to walk again. I know this is the right thing to do, I am just a bit scared about meeting people in society, people who are blinded by the Machine.'

The Master says: 'Yet you have told me that you will do anything to be part of the process of freeing this planet from the Machine. You have also said you are willing to do what it takes to compensate for your past actions, such as killing other people.'

'As you will recall, I told you that you need to do three things, namely invoke light, shift your sense of self and give service to life. The key to overcoming your identification with the separate self is to get to a point where you realize that life is not about *you* anymore. Your life is no longer revolving around protecting the wounds, prides and sensitivities of the separate self. You have depersonalized your personal life. Your life is about becoming one with the whole, and this requires giving service to the whole.'

The importance of service

'We have entered a new age where being a spiritual person cannot be done only by living in a retreat. In the time you have been here, I have told several long-term students that they needed to go out into society for a time in order to rise to a higher level of their path. You are now at that point.'

'You will not free yourself from the remnants of your separate self and you will not free yourself from your past actions by remaining in this retreat. You will do so only by going out and giving service to life. For you to go into a program of receiving an artificial leg and being retrained is not about you. It is about you giving service to the people you will meet, even thought they think they are serving you. They *are* also serving you, and that is how you grow together.'

'There are many people in embodiment today who have volunteered to be born into difficult circumstances or to experience them later in life. These people are the forerunners for a shift in the collective consciousness. They have volunteered to take on great physical challenges in order to demonstrate that material conditions cannot define you as a spiritual being. You can still manifest a more spiritual life regardless of the physical conditions.'

'You are one of these people. This does not mean it was a certainty that you would lose a leg, but it was a possibility. You were meant to be in a war situation and demonstrate that you can rise above this and become a forerunner for peace, a Warrior of Peace.'

'My Son, no true master wants his or her students to become dependent upon the teacher. I have given you enough teachings and tools that you have established some contact to your I AM Presence and spiritual teachers. You do not need to remain in this ashram because we will all be with you as you go out. You cannot be separated from us by time and space because we are beyond time and space and so is the Conscious You—when it knows who it is.'

'I look forward to seeing you come back here, walking on two legs. I also look forward to seeing whom you might bring with you upon your return.'

The Warrior returns

More than a year passes. One day the Master and his students are eating lunch in the dining hall when the door is opened. A man dressed in an impeccable business suit walks through the door. He is cleanly shaved and walks with a barely perceptible limp. The students all look up, but it takes them a few seconds to recognize the Warrior.

The Warrior walks in and behind him follows a beautiful women who is almost nine months pregnant. The Warrior looks all of the students in the eye as he slowly walks towards

20 | *The Warrior Leaves and Returns*

the Master's table. Tears of joy are running down his cheeks and the same happens to those students who knew the Warrior before. As he stops before the Master, he must take some time before he is able to speak.

'Master, I know you know everything that has happened to me, for I have felt your Presence with me always. Yet I felt there was value in coming here physically and presenting you with my wife and our coming child. I know you know how profoundly grateful I am, but my wife and I both want to express our gratitude for what you have done for me and for bringing us together.'

The Master wipes a tear and says: 'My Son, I thank you for bringing my daughter here physically. I know you will both be busy with raising a family and ministering to life. I want you to know that when you come to the point in your lives when it is time to withdraw from society for a time, you are welcome here.'

The Warrior says with a glimpse in his eyes: 'Master, will you promise to be here no matter how long that takes?'

The Master answers with a smile: 'I will indeed be here, for through various forms, I am with you always.'

Note: For the spiritual tools recommended by the Master, see: *www.transcendencetoolbox.com*.

www.ingramcontent.com/pod-product-compliance
Lightning Source LLC
Chambersburg PA
CBHW021148160426
43194CB00007B/731